Reviews of this Book...

"Provides much useful information to the prospective patient and goes some distance in explaining what to look for and what to avoid. I am pleased to recommend it."

Hans H. Strupp, Ph.D., Distinguished Professor of Psychology, Vanderbilt University; co-author of *Psychotherapy for Better or Worse: The Problem of Negative Effects*.

"Dr. Striano has documented in a consumer report study a variety of 'horror stories' of the type that are often shared privately among clients and professionals but are rarely published."

Allen E. Bergin, Ph.D., co-author of *Handbook of Psychotherapy and Behavior Change;* Director, Institute for Studies in Values and Human Behavior, Brigham Young University.

"Down-to-earth and of real use for the consumer."

Donald K. Freedheim, Ph.D., Editor, *Psychotherapy: Theory/Research/Practice/Training,* journal of the Division of Psychotherapy, American Psychological Association.

"We have guidebooks for choosing everything from cars to insurance policies. Finally, we have help to find a good psychotherapist. For many consumers this book could be a godsend."

Linda F. Golodner, Executive Director, National Consumers League, founded in 1899

"Highly recommended and long overdue. A useful book for individuals who are seeking a psychotherapist. The best defense against incompetence in this field is an educated consumer."

E. Fuller Torrey, M.D., clinical and research psychiatrist in Washington D.C., author of *Witchdoctors and Psychiatrists.* For four years he was Special Assistant to the Director of the National Institute of Mental Health, he has been a contributing editor to popular magazine *Psychology Today,* and he has been nominated for a National Book Critics Circle award.

"A great idea . . . should prove a valuable resource . . . might even have spinoff for initiatives in other parts of the world."

Godfrey T. Barrett-Lennard, Director, Centre for Studies in Human Relations, West Perth, Australia; author of the "Relationship Inventory," the major questionnaire used in researching the client's perception of the therapeutic relationship.

"Dr. Judi Striano is one of those rare combinations of rigorous scientist with the intuition of an artist. Her book reflects both elements."

Harold Greenwald, Ph.D., Founder and Director, Direct Decision Therapy Institute, San Diego, California; President, Division of Humanistic Psychology, American Psychological Association; author of many book and co-author of *The Happy Person.*

"This is a scholarly and serious research project done in an excellent and professional manner in a vastly neglected area."

Lawrence LeShan, Ph.D., President,
Association for Humanistic Psychology;
author of *You Can Fight For Your Life: Emotional Factors in the Causation of Cancer, The Mechanic and the Gardener: Making the Most of the Holistic Revolution in Medicine, Counseling the Dying, How to Meditate, Alternate Realities,* and other books.

How To Find A *<u>Good</u>* *Psychotherapist: A Consumer Guide*

Judi Striano, Ph.D.

PROFESSIONAL PRESS
P.O. Box 50343
Santa Barbara, California 93150

 For information write to Professional Press, P.O. Box 50343, Santa Barbara, California 93150.

FIRST EDITION

Library of Congress
Cataloging-in-Publication Data

Striano, Judith Cecere, 1941-
How to find a good psychotherapist.

Bibliography: p.
1. Psychotherapist and patient.
2. Psychotherapy—Evaluation.
3. Psychotherapy patients—Interviews.
4. Consumer education. I. Title.
RC480.8.S77 1987 616.89'14 87-61143
ISBN 0-943659-00-0

Contents

Dedicated to

Harold Greenwald, Ph.D.
For his creativity in the design
of this study
and for his friendship

Acknowledgements

This book would not have been possible without
the contributions of the following people:
Godfrey T. Barrett-Lennard, Ph.D.
Allen E. Bergin, Ph.D.
Ted Berkman, writer
Rodney Davis, Ph.D.
Harold Greenwald, Ph.D.
Frederic M. Hudson, Ph.D.
Lawrence LeShan, Ph.D.
William Mariano, attorney
Martin F. O'Malley, ACSW
Hans S. Strupp, Ph.D.

The success of this study is largely due
to the clients who so courageously
allowed me to interview them.

CHAPTER 1

Shopping Around: What To Look For And Avoid

I have worked as a psychotherapist for twenty years in clinics where psychotherapists sit with clients behind closed doors without revealing what they do. How many professions enjoy such privacy?

Through the years I have heard story after story from clients about psychotherapists who have helped them and psychotherapists who have not helped them, or have even harmed them, and I have wished I could do something about quality control of psychotherapy. The purpose of this book is to educate consumers by reporting both positive and negative experiences, so psychotherapy clients can have a better shot at getting the help they want.

Consumer magazines and consumer advocates guide you in comparison shopping for cars, tuna fish, and ice cream, so you can get the best quality at the best prices. We're told about the best restaurants and the worst movies. But, there are no consumer reports for finding a *good* psychotherapist. This is the first.

People in the process of looking for a psychotherapist are often distressed and searching for help and are not in the best situation to be able to adequately make good judgments about anything, including choosing a good psychotherapist. Add to this the unknown character of what's out there, the fact that effective psychotherapy is an elusive area to evaluate. The competence of a medical doctor, for example, is easier to determine. If his diagnosis is wrong, this can often be determined using a microscope or x-ray. If the medication he prescribes is wrong or he makes an error in surgery, you'll know this too. But, it's much more difficult to determine injury by a psychotherapist. The third problem is that the whole nature of the process of psychotherapy is not like any other treatment. It's a process of interplay of two forces—the therapist and the client. For example, you don't necessarily have to have a lawyer who matches well with your personality. You and he don't need to get involved personally, as you and your psychotherapist do. You *hire* a lawyer who is a good *technician*.

Looking in the Yellow Pages of your telephone book won't help you find a good psychotherapist. Schools granting degrees to people who become psychotherapists, state licensing boards, professional organizations, focus more on finding out about academic success—scores on exams and grade point averages—than they do on finding out about the personal qualities of the therapist. And, if he's been in an office working individually with his clients during his training, what do his supervisors actually know about what he does? The same is true for the professional organizations. How does any therapist know what any other therapist really does?

Most clients believe that any psychotherapist—just because he is a psychotherapist—is a capable "expert" and emotionally very well put together, rather than just a person with his own problems. A therapist is, of course, just a person, and cannot separate himself, personally, from the techniques he learns to use in therapy. And, the techniques of therapy are not all that help. The *person* of the therapist, who he is—his perceptions, feelings, thinking, sense of reality, anything that affects you—can be helpful or not helpful. The environment he creates by being the person he is, and the relationship you both create by having your own unique personalities, can be helpful or not helpful. Is your therapist helpful for you, or should you look for another? This book will teach you how to decide.

A *good* psychotherapist as described in this book will not help every client, because shopping for a psychotherapist also involves finding one who's right for you. Some people just don't "fit" together well, don't get along with each other, as we all know. And, unfortunately, psychotherapy doesn't help every client. We don't know enough yet about what makes people distressed or how to help everyone.

Some clients would get worse with any therapist as well as without a therapist. Don't believe any therapist who *guarantees* he can help you. He can't possibly know that.

This book is divided into four chapters. In Chapter 1 consumers who have had both helpful and unhelpful individual psychotherapists report their experiences and compare what each of their therapists did, how each was different, and tell you what they recommend you look for and avoid when you comparison shop. In Chapter 2 consumers tell *how* therapists help, what they *do* that helps, and how their lives have changed as a result. Examples in Chapter 3 about what the buyer should beware of, how psychotherapists can harm you, will protect you. In Chapter 4 we give you a checklist you can use to rate your psychotherapist on qualities that make the difference between helpful and not helpful psychotherapy.

Before you decide to look for a psychotherapist you should rule out possible physical causes for your distress. Many so-called *psychological* problems really have *physiological* causes. I recently had a 73 year old client complaining of depression, fatigue, forgetfulness, and other symptoms. It would have been easy for me to dismiss some of her symptoms as inevitable for someone her age, but this is an inaccurate, commonly held myth. It would also have been easy for me to think that her reactions to unpleasant experiences in her life were the reason. But, instead of diagnosing her with a psychological label, I asked her to consult a medical doctor, an endocrinologist I know who has a good reputation for competent work. He found she has an underactive thyroid. She now takes thyroid replacement hormones, her symptoms have disappeared, and she doesn't need a psychotherapist.

Just because a psychiatrist is a medical doctor, *don't* assume that he has fully evaluated your problem and ruled out all possible physical conditions that could be causing your symptoms. Even though psychiatrists are medical doctors, they usually don't practice as "real doctors." They usually don't examine their clients physically. And they often leave their medical knowledge, skills, and practice behind them, preferring not to have stethoscopes, blood-drawing equipment, examining tables, or any medical equipment, except their prescription pads, and many prefer to believe that their clients' problems are "psychogenic," that is, caused by emotional disturbances. In fact, one psychiatrist I know about calls himself a "bio-psychiatrist," to convey that before he diagnoses or begins therapy with a client he carefully looks first for physical illnesses that may be causing the symptoms. Even if a psychiatrist were to examine you physically, don't trust that his diagnosis is accurate. A high percentage of people have physical illnesses that are misdiagnosed, that are causing their distress. Some of these people may even be committed to psychiatric hospitals. Unfortunately, even internists and other "real doctors," have an extraordinarily high rate of this misdiagnosis. I know someone who consulted 37 physicians before her physical problem was diagnosed. All the other doctors had told her that she was emotionally disturbed, not physically ill—and they were wrong.

Just because you are considering beginning psychotherapy doesn't mean that you need it. However, many psychotherapists will assume you need it because you show up in their offices as possible clients. Many mental health professionals are what I call "pathology hunters," that is, they have a bias toward interpreting behavior as "sick" rather than healthy. And arriving at the admitting unit of a psychiatric hospital will almost always get you a pathological diagnosis you don't deserve and will probably get you admitted as a patient because the staff may think that just because you are in the admitting unit of a psychiatric hospital you are psychologically disturbed. See chapter 3 about an experiment by D.L. Rosenhan, professor of psychology and law at Stanford University, in which he and others researched this personally when they were wrongfully diagnosed and mistakenly admitted to psychiatric hospitals.

Don't be discouraged if what you've read so far in this book leads you to be pessimistic about your search for a helpful therapist. You *can* take charge of this search, even if you are distressed. And you *can* find a therapist who's right for you.

Here are some definitions that will help you know the differences among mental health professionals who are psychotherapists. For years psychotherapists have traditionally been psychiatrists, psychologists, or social workers.

A psychiatrist is a medical doctor (M.D.) whose training is in medicine with four years in medical school, a one year internship (supervised work experience), and then a three or four year residency training program in psychiatry. A medical license is required to practice psychiatry, but the title "psychiatrist" can be used by any medical doctor without approval from anyone. Some psychiatrists are "board certified" by the American Board of Psychiatry and Neurology. See explanation below of the fact that approval by such boards does *not* necessarily mean the psychiatrist is competent. A psychiatrist is the only psychotherapist who can give you a prescription for medication because he is a medical doctor.

A psychologist has a doctorate—Doctor of Philosophy (Ph.D.), Doctor of Psychology (Psy.D.), or Doctor of Education (Ed.D.)—although some states license psychologists with a Master of Arts (M.A.). The psychologist with a master's degree has two years of graduate courses and may or may not have other requirements or training. A psychologist with a doctorate has four years of graduate school courses, a research study called a dissertation is required, a one year internship (supervised work experience), and some have post-doctoral supervised work experience. Most state laws require a doctorate, two years supervised experience, and passing grades on more than one examination covering all aspects of psychology and psychotherapy for certification or licensing. Some psychologists were "grandfathered in," which means that they were given certification or licenses to practice under a "grandfather clause" even though they may not have had all the requirements necessary to be eligible for certification or licensing but they were already in practice—were working as psychologists—before the laws were created.

Psychologists may have degrees in other areas of psychology, such as experimental psychology or school psychology, but only a psychologist with a degree in "clinical psychology" is trained to do psychotherapy, and a psychologist with a degree in "counseling psychology" is trained to do counseling, with the distinction between psychotherapy and counseling not so clearly defined or so extremely separate. Some psychologists have approval from the American Board of Examiners in Professional Psychology or are listed in the National Register of Health Service Providers in Psychology, but see the explanation below of the fact that approval by such groups does *not* necessarily mean the psychologist is competent. In fact, the National Register refuses to list some graduates of regionally accredited schools who are licensed in their states, members of the American Psychological Association, and meet all the "requirements" for inclusion in the National Register.

A master's degree social worker (M.S.W.) is trained in a two year graduate school also involving "field placement " (supervised work experience). Very few social workers have a doctorate (D.S.W.) in social work, although these degrees do exist. Not all states have laws regulating the title of social worker, but many states do, requiring a passing grade on an examination to be "certified" and to use the title "CSW," or "Certified Social Worker." Some social workers were "grandfathered in," which means they were certified under a "grandfather clause," even though they may not have had the qualifications necessary to be eligible for this certification, because they were in practice—were working as social workers—before the laws were created. They may also be certified by the Academy of Certified Social Workers (ACSW). See explanation below of the fact that "approval" by such groups does *not* necessarily mean the social worker is competent. Not all MSW social workers are trained for clinical or psychiatric work. Some people who do not have MSWs or any degrees call themselves social workers because they work in various agencies that provide "social services" to people.

Membership in the American Psychiatric Association, American Psychological Association, National Association of Social Workers, or approval by the American Board of Psychiatry and Neurology, the American Board of Examiners in Professional Psychology, the Academy of Certified Social Workers, or listing in the National Register of Health Service Providers in Psychology or the Register of Clinical Social Workers does *not* necessarily mean that the therapist is competent. It only means that he has passed some sort of examination, and some group of people working in the same profession have allowed him to be accepted into their "club." Some of the club members organize for the purpose of sharing ideas and working collaboratively with others and for the purpose of quality control of their profession. But, unfortunately, many professionals have their own personal and professional preferences and biases and want to prevent others who don't agree with their ideas from becoming affiliated with them. Other members may want to keep the supply and demand at a ratio that is financially profitable for them to be sure there aren't so many psychotherapists that they won't have enough clients to be able to earn a living for themselves. The organization is, then, a "trade union," or "guild" protecting the income of its members, rather than a regulatory agency protecting the consumers of services, and anyone who doesn't belong may have difficulty finding work, and insurance companies may not consider them legitimate and may not reimburse their clients because they don't belong to this exclusive group.

Some of these professionals may also attend a "psychotherapy training institute" for training in psychotherapy, or a "psychoanalytic training institute" for training in psychoanalysis (form of psychotherapy originated by Sigmund Freud and which now has versions founded by others). But this additional training is *not* required, does *not* mean these therapists are more competent in psychotherapy than whose who do not attend these institutions. It only means that they are learning to do psychotherapy or psychoanalysis using the particular theory and style of the administrators of the institute. They pay the institute for this training, and the institute refers clients to them, which is of great help in establishing their own businesses. Some institutes may also accept psychotherapy students who do not have the degrees or training required by their states for licenses or certification as psychotherapists, and are not connected to the various professional associations, boards, and listings we have discussed.

Besides the traditional professionals we've talked about you may find a psychotherapist belonging to one of the groups defined below.

The term "marriage counselor" is not legally regulated by most states. But there are some graduate programs in marriage, family, and child counseling, and some states have rules controlling the practice of "MFCCs," but admission to these examinations may be open to people from a variety of professional backgrounds. I know someone with a Ph.D. in clinical psychology who was recently admitted to and passed the MFCC examination in New Jersey. The descriptions "family counselor," "family therapist," and "child counselor" are not regulated legally.

"School psychologist" is a title controlled by law with state licensing or certification requirements of education, experience, and examination. School psychologists generally work in schools with children who have learning or behavior problems and refer them to other professionals for remedial help and psychotherapy.

People calling themselves "counselors," "guidance counselors," "vocational counselors," "career counselors" usually can do so without anyone's permission because most states don't have rules for these areas yet. But I do know, for example, that Texas has a controlled "professional counselor" title, and some other states may have their own additional titles. Another example is that California requires anyone calling himself a career counselor to take the same examination used for employment agency counselors, but New York State allows anyone to say he is a career counselor.

Anyone can use the title "sex therapist." Be especially careful that this person has some reasonable, professional, licensed connection with medicine or psychology, although, as I have said, you can never be sure you are adequately protected even if a therapist has credentials. Use good judgment in your choice and gather enough information to be an informed consumer.

Each state legislates its own rules about licensing and certification. There are no standard licensing procedures or rules throughout the country. It is important to understand that there is no one licensing group for psychotherapists. In the United States each state requires physicians and nurses to be licensed. These licenses, however, are to practice medicine. They are *not* licenses to practice psychotherapy. Psychologists must be licensed in most states, social workers in many, and a few states have begun to license marriage and family counselors. But even though all these people may have licenses and may work as psychotherapists, they are given licenses by separate licensing boards. E. Fuller Torrey, clinical and research psychiatrist in Washington, D.C., who for four years was Special Assistant to the Director of the National Institute of Mental Health, has been a contributing editor to popular magazine Psychology Today, and has been nominated for a National Book Critics Circle award, says in his book *Witchdoctors and Psychiatrists: The Common Roots of Psychotherapy and Its Future:*

> "Moving toward a system of licensing and accreditation of psychotherapists would require cooperation among the various disciplines that constitute the psychotherapy pool. . . . The prospect of such cooperation is not bright at present, when the leading disciplines—the psychiatrists, psychologists, and social workers—are engaged in constant warfare against each other as each tries to protect and enlarge its turf. A *Washington Post* article in 1985 [by Goleman—April 30th] headlined 'Social Workers Vault into a Leading Role in Psychotherapy: Psychiatrists and Psychologists Defend Territory as Competition Increases.'"

Used to be that psychiatrists, the medical doctors, were considered to be the only psychotherapists. Then psychologists invaded their territory, and more recently psychiatric social workers have been moving in on both. And all three are trying to prevent marriage and family counselors from joining them. There's lots of money to be made in the psychotherapy trade and there are great rewards for those who can take over part of the market. Becoming eligible for "third party payments," which means that their services are reimbursed by insurance programs, is important in attracting clients, and this issue is a constant point of contention among all.

You may find people with other degrees or even without licenses, sometimes sanctioned by psychotherapy or psychoanalytic training institutes they've attended, and other people who call themselves psychotherapists but do not have credentials—degrees or training or anyone's approval—who just work independently of any organized group.

Within agencies such as hospitals, many staff who are nurses or "psychiatric nurses," and even "therapy aides" who are called "paraprofessionals" might be called psychotherapists within their agencies even though they may have little or no formal education in psychotherapy and may not be licensed or certified to practice privately outside of their agencies.

There are no laws preventing a minister, priest, rabbi, etc., from using the title "pastoral counselor," and use of this title does not mean he has training in counseling or psychotherapy.

Education alone does not make a person a good psychotherapist, but of course, the more complete and longer the training—high quality training—the more knowledge and possibly better technical skills of the therapist. But even though some therapists with less thorough academic work and fewer years training or no formal education might be better therapists for you because they have a natural talent for the work or healthier personalities or they're just right for you, we still recommend that you first look for a licensed professional and then explore his personal and professional qualities looking for the helpful characteristics described in this book.

About charges. What's reasonable and what's outrageous? Psychiatrists charge the highest fees, with psychologists usually in second place, MSWs third, and MFCCs possibly less. But paying a high fee does *not* mean you're getting better therapy. It's not like comparing the high quality of Mercedes Benz or Rolls Royce with less expensive cars. I once heard two people comparing their therapists' fees, with one client justifying the extraordinarily high fees her therapist charged because his office was on the seventeenth floor, the penthouse, in a building on Central Park West in New York City, and the therapist, therefore, evidently in her estimation, had more prestige and status. My therapist isn't better than your therapist if mine is on the seventeenth floor and yours on the third. The saying that you get what you pay for is not necessarily true about psychotherapists. A therapist usually charges higher fees if he has a "good reputation." But, his "reputation" might be built on the fact that he is known for his writings, that he graduated from or teaches in a prestigious school, that he is the president of a professional psychological organization, or maybe that he has a luxury office in an exclusive part of town and charges high fees, or he has famous people as clients, or he's charming or entertaining, etc. But his writing and teaching may not be worthwhile, and even if they are that doesn't mean he is a good psychotherapist or that he would be right for you. Graduating from a prestigious school is possible if he can read books and pass exams. Being president of a professional psychological organization may just mean he is a good politician or very ambitious or likes to be a leader or to have power. About the luxury office—lots of people would be impressed if you tell them you bought your dress at Bloomingdale's, Bergdorf Goodman, or Neiman Marcus. High fees may mean he has a lavish lifestyle. Having famous clients doesn't mean he's effective. Famous people are just people too, and especially when they're distressed their judgment may not be better than anyone else's. You want someone whose reputation is built on the fact that he effectively helps people through their crises, that he is an effective psychotherapist. Also, some therapists who build good reputations for the right reasons, that is they initially are effective therapists, may get caught up with their fame, believe they are truly great men, and lose some of the qualities responsible for their effectiveness. Or they may "burn out," that is lose interest in their work.

Unfortunately, you probably won't find a therapist in private practice today for less than $30 an hour. I think you should avoid anyone who charges more than $75, especially if you're paying for his outrageously expensive living. That's not fair or kind. I recently heard about a therapist in Los Angeles who charges $175 an hour. An "hour," by the way, may actually be only 45 minutes. Ask the therapist about this. Hospital outpatient departments and public and private agencies may charge less, but then you're involved with bureaucracy with inflexible administrative structures and procedures and billing departments, instead of a private situation with more informal arrangements which are less intrusive and where you're much less visible to the world. There may possibly be more safety with agencies because other staff are present and you are not entirely alone with a therapist in private practice in his very private office. But, often agency staff don't report harmful psychotherapists even if they know about them. It is my experience that insurance companies are more likely to reimburse you for therapy with psychiatrists and psychologists than with other psychotherapists. Read your policy and telephone your insurance company and ask if you will be reimbursed for therapy with the therapist you've chosen *before* you begin therapy. I know about a woman who just assumed her insurance would pay, but after submitting her bill for months of appointments she was told the company would not reimburse her for therapy with that particular therapist.

If the therapist wants you to pay him for every visit even if you cancel because you are ill, have a conflicting appointment, are on vacation, or if he wants you to pay him in advance for your visits, consider finding someone else. His priority is a predictable income. It's not you and your distress. As one consumer said, a therapist who didn't help him wanted "an annuity, not a client." Of course, you can't expect him to keep an appointment time available for you if you frequently cancel or just don't show and he is consistently without payment for the time set aside for you.

Consumers often don't like paying for the first visit while they're shopping for a therapist, just as they don't have to pay to try on a dress or test drive a car. This can be costly. Given the unique situation of psychotherapy, that it may continue for weeks or months or years, and involves interplay among personal qualities of the participants as well as professional knowledge and skills necessary for understanding the kinds of problems of the client, such as marital, sexual, substance abuse, if a therapist charges for the first visit, the consumer could spend much money while interviewing prospective therapists. And how is it possible to determine in less than an hour if the therapist really knows about treatment of the client's unique problem, and if the two participants can work well together personally? Although, ideally, our recommendation would be that you look for therapists who do not charge for the first visit, we cannot recommend this. Therapists should not be expected to give away their time free. Physicians and lawyers don't give away "free samples" of their work. And some therapists may even use the prospect of a free sample to attract you into their offices.

A way around this problem of costly first visits when you're shopping is to try to find out as much as possible in a phone conversation or in a brief face-to-face interview *before* making an appointment for your first visit. Ask about the therapist's qualifications, training, his theories about what causes people to be distressed, what kinds of therapy he practices, what he thinks might work best for you, how long he expects you will be in therapy, if he's had other clients with similar problems as yours and understands the problem enough so this area is considered a "specialty" for him, fees, how long his waiting list is if he has one, at what times and how often he is available to see you. Then, if your first visit is used for a professional assessment of your problems and plans for therapy, you may feel that is worth paying for, that it is a billable professional service. One of the reasons why you wouldn't want to pay for the first visit is if the therapist rejects you—does not want you as a client because he too is "shopping around" for clients and he does not choose you. You especially wouldn't want to pay if he doesn't choose you because you are not personally appealing to him. Another reason he might not want you is if you can't afford his fees. He should have told you about his fees and he should have known about your financial circumstances before he gave you an appointment.

As you shop for a therapist, you should interview several, asking each to describe his style of therapy, how he works with clients, what he thinks is important, how he would pursue what he intends. If a therapist refuses to give you an interview, to answer your questions, except those that are too personal, find another. Try to find therapists who have credentials: degrees from accredited schools, state licenses, membership in professional organizations of high quality. But, having all these still doesn't mean he or she is a *good* therapist. If he can read books and pass exams, he can get a degree. He can find someone to supervise him and recommend him for a state license, and we already know he can pass exams, so he'll probably pass the licensing exam too. And the same for the professional organizations. Once he's established, chances are that no other professional will want to take all the risks involved to challenge his competence.

Asking your family physician to refer you to a psychotherapist is not the best way to find a *good* one. Physicians may not understand the necessary personal qualities and professional skills of effective psychotherapy. And they may not know about the therapist's professional skills or how he relates as a person with his clients. Some physicians may try to match the client with a therapist who has experience and success working with clients with similar difficulties, and a therapist with a personality compatible to the clients. But physicians tend to refer to therapists they know personally or those with nearby offices. Also, a physician will most often refer to a psychiatrist (who is also a physician) instead of a psychologist or psychiatric social worker.

If you phone professional societies to which psychiatrists, psychologists, and psychiatric social workers belong, you will probably be offered names of three therapists, but you will *not* be given ratings of their competence. You also will not be given the kind of information you need to be able to make an informed decision if you phone a so-called "referral agency." And these sources will never tell you about his personal qualities, and they don't know if you and he will have healthy "rapport" and work together well.

The best approach is to ask people you know who've been in therapy to recommend therapists for you to interview. As E. Fuller Torrey writes, therapists they would rate high on a scale of "would-you-want-to-go-to-this-person-if-you-had-problems." Evaluate your interview experiences by talking with other clients, preferably clients who have had both helpful and not helpful therapy. They're not hard to find. I can envision consumer groups in each town. banding together and rating local therapists and publishing the top and lowest rated in the daily newspaper. No one rates psychotherapists. I think we should. We'll do this in Chapter 4.

A good idea when you're shopping is to take someone whose judgment you trust with you to the first interview, someone, ideally who has himself had both a helpful and unhelpful therapist, so he knows the difference. You'll have the benefit of the perceptions of two people and increase your chances of choosing someone who will help and not harm you. If the therapist will not allow this, insisting he see you alone, leave immediately and cross him off your list.

You can't expect to know all you'd like to know about the therapists you interview after your first visit of less than an hour. You will have to make a tentative decision to begin therapy with someone and continue to evaluate information about him and the results and effectiveness of your therapy and revise your decisions after a few sessions. You've got to give it time. You wouldn't marry someone you'd known for less than an hour. Also, you may feel worse before you feel better, and this may not have anything to do with the therapist. Talking about your problems and changing your life patterns are not easy and may not be pleasant for you. But you *don't* necessarily have to suffer a lot as I discuss in Chapter 3.

It is important that you "comparison shop" rather than choosing only one therapist and staying with him and then blaming him or yourself if you're not helped. Psychotherapy is a buyer's market and you have lots of therapists to choose from.

Feeling "comfortable" with the therapist, that you "fit" together well in a healthy and productive fit, is also very important. But, if you're too comfortable you may not be motivated to change.

Remember, that it is, after all, the client's experience that counts. You are the best judge of the effectiveness of therapy. You know if you are a satisfied "customer." As the consumer of services, the client must have a voice in evaluating his psychotherapist.

Many clients who have negative experiences are reluctant to try again with another therapist. The clients heard from in this book did try again, then had positive experiences, and know the differences between the two. Read the recommendations of one consumer:

1. Look for: "The individual's background in terms of education, philosophy, internship, the environment in which the therapist operates from. And, certainly, a gut feeling after interviewing a therapist. I would interview therapists—sit and talk with them about how I feel, what my needs are, and how they respond to what I say, if I feel comfortable or not comfortable, how the person is about money. I would be turned off to a therapist who charged for the initial session. I think it's unfair. There's a degree of shopping in looking for a therapist. I don't think people should be charged for information."

Author's note: See above in this chapter for discussion of fees. I will repeat again here that although, ideally, our recommendation would be that you look for therapists who do not charge for the first visit, we cannot recommend this. Therapists should not be expected to give away their time free. Physicians and lawyers don't given away "free samples" of their work. And some therapists may even use the prospect of a free sample to attract you into their offices. Try to find out as much as possible in a phone conversation or in a brief face-to-face interview *before* making an appointment for your first visit. Ask about the therapist's qualifications, training, his theories about what causes people to be distressed, what kinds of therapy he practices, what he thinks might work best for you, how long he expects you will be in therapy, if he's had other clients with similar problems as yours and if he can consider this a "specialty" area for him, fees, how long his waiting list is if he has one, at what times and how often he is available to see you. Then, if your first visit is used for a professional assessment of your problems and plans for therapy, you may feel that is worth paying for, that it is a billable professional service. One of the reasons you would not want to pay for the first visit is if the therapist rejects you—does not want you as a client because he too is "shopping around" for clients and he does not choose you. You especially wouldn't want to pay if he doesn't choose you because you are not personally appealing to him. Another reason is if you can't afford his fees—he should have told you about his fees and he should have known about your financial circumstances before he gave you an appointment.

Another consumer tells us:

2. *Look for:* "Do some research about what you're looking for. Have an understanding of what you're looking for—what your expectations are. Can the therapist provide that for you? Speak with people who may have been in the situation. But, don't select blindly or think that if somebody has a Ph.D. or is a clinical psychologist that he knows what he's doing. Because very often he does not. And understand that being a therapist is a profession and has nothing to do with who the individual is in terms of his own life. People believe that if you're a therapist, you're together. They really want to believe that because how can you go sit and talk about your stuff unless you really feel that the other person is together. And have a sense that the therapist understands the difference between intervention and interference. When a therapist tells a client what to do and how to do it—that's interference."

Avoid: "A therapist who interferes, who isn't competent, or is pushing for business. Has no tangible credentials. And just my sense after asking questions and listening to how the therapist speaks. And maybe eye contact, body language. And it would come together. And whether I can work with that person comfortably."

Another suggests:

3. ***Look for:*** "First of all, shop for a therapist the way you shop for anything else that's important in your life. If you would comparison shop for a car or a dress or a pair of shoes or anything else, you should do the same with a therapist. You are spending your money for a service, and you have the same rights to good service as you do for anything else. The people who are therapists are not God.

They are people with a certain amount of training and different people have different training and what they sell is themselves and a service and their interpretation of their service and the knowledge and experience that they've gained. And the same way that a dress can be poorly made and a car can have defects in it, so any therapist can have his or her flaws. The way that one car or one dress may fit one person and not another person, in the same way, one therapist can fit one person and not another person. It doesn't mean that that therapist is a bad therapist in an overall objective sense, but maybe he's not right for you, and you shouldn't feel terrible. You don't feel terrible if one dress is not your color or style, and you shouldn't feel terrible if one therapist is not your style. Someone who would be able to communicate with you. Therapy is a communicating skill. Of course, you have to communicate something about what's going on with you, but the therapist has to communicate something back in terms of what he sees about what's going on and in such a way that you are able to use it. If that is not happening, for whatever reason, whether he's speaking a different language, or he just doesn't care to communicate, or he just doesn't understand the particular problem that you have, then you have to find somebody else. A person who is able to fit into the kinds of problems and situations that you have. There has to be a relationship, a trusting relationship. He has to be able to establish a relationship that's going to feel comfortable to you, where you're going to be able to feel safe enough to communicate what's going on."

Avoid: "Anyone who makes you feel bad. The purpose of therapy is to feel better about yourself and to be able to function better, and anyone who encourages or elicits more negative feelings than when you went in is not doing his job. Someone who cannot relate to you either because of some kind of deficit or just that he is a different personality type—his manner of relating does not fit with yours. You may get a great therapist. But you may be a very shy, retiring little girl type and get a big blustery guy who is going to overwhelm you and you just may not feel safe in terms of revealing things about yourself. It could be the other way around. You could be a truck driver who comes in to work out marital problems and you get a nice little girl type who's a great therapist but is very, very meek and you don't interact well. There have to be some kinds of paths that the two of you have in common that form a kind of human bridge. If you were so different or on such different wavelengths that you don't have the initial points to make contact, then you may eventually, if you spend ten years in therapy, work those out, but that's kind of wasteful. You might be able to find somebody you click with better."

More from consumers:

4. Avoid: "People who tell you what to do. People who tell you 'I know I can help you.' People who say 'You should' or 'You shouldn't'—key words. People who have only one approach. For example, therapists who say they're 'Freudian,' and they say 'Lie down on the couch and talk.' They want you to free associate for forty minutes."

Author's note: You must beware of therapists who guarantee that they can help you. Don't believe them. No therapist can be sure he can help you, and if he promises you help he is violating ethical standards, and if he is a licensed psychologist, psychiatrist, social worker, etc., and belongs to professional societies, he could lose his license and professional memberships. Beware of therapists who tell you what you should do. They're not helping you become independent and may be leading you down the wrong path. Therapists who are rigid, not flexible, and who use only one therapeutic approach for all their clients, believing that they have found the only correct and effective way, are obviously not open to other possibilities, and you do not want someone with such unrealistic attitudes.

5. Look for: "Get a therapist from a recommendation from someone you know and trust to make a good recommendation. Formal education is very important — academic degree. But that's not enough. It's important that he has had his own personal therapy so he understands himself and doesn't inflict his problems on his clients. I doubt that the therapist who didn't help me had therapy. Be sure that a chummy relationship does not develop because I think familiarity gets in the way of the objectivity that's necessary. I would run from a therapist who would introduce his personal life. You're the weak one. He's supposed to know better. Unfortunately, very often there's a role reversal. The client becomes the crutch for the therapist. But not a person I can run all over and destroy. Don't let him dominate you either. I have to feel free to call him on the phone occasionally, but I don't want to be encouraged to do it all the time because that's making me dependent on him. I would run from a therapist who would introduce me to any other client of his for any reason. There's a rapport that no one can quantify. It's a qualitative thing. You must feel comfortable. But, be cautious. You don't necessarily have to fit like a glove like I did with the one who didn't help me. There must be respect so you will feel free to talk with this person. Someone who respects you for whatever you are, and recognizes your good points. I thought my helpful therapist was professional and knew what he was doing, and I respected him. You must be able to confide in him. I couldn't work with someone who was in his early twenties, who didn't have experience."

Author's note: I recommend not choosing a therapist who is just beginning to practice, and doesn't have a lot of experience, especially if you are in crisis with a serious problem.

6. Look for: "Essentially, I would want some kind of balance between a human being and someone who could guide a client through the difficult things that people have to go through. A kind of almighty gardener who can really help him to grow, to blossom. I would like clients to find out what that therapist is like and see if that person is right for them. Not everyone is going to develop a positive relationship with everyone else. There are some people who just won't get along and it's a pity to go for a year or so and find out that you're not. The professions are so imposing. An edifice. How do you go into that edifice and kind of poke around and ask questions and say 'Are you going to be right for me?' I don't know if you're going to be right for me. I wouldn't go to someone who is rich and who is a famous therapist. Because it's very high power.

They're inclined to take themselves too seriously and become the cardboard image. I'd look for people who are connected with some kind of professional body so you can see where they're coming from and what kind of training they've had. People who are human. People who are able to talk with another person so there's some real communication going on between the two people. This takes a lot of exploring and courage. Clients who are beginning in therapy quite often don't have that kind of facility. I certainly didn't have real communication. It would have taken an immense amount of courage to be able to ask those kinds of questions like 'Who are you?' 'Do you think you can treat me?' I was scared."

Avoid: "Avoid people who seem to have no professional connection. Avoid people who want to make a lot of money out of you. Avoid charlatans. Avoid people who are slick. Avoid someone who gives you a lot of easy answers. There are some people who are very charismatic, who are very powerful kinds of personalities. I think that has its place in some kinds of treatment. It may have its place in treatment of psychotic people. But, a person who is going to relate to you with this charisma, with a personality that kind of mesmerizes you, is really not going to help you deal with reality when that person is not around and really prepare you for autonomy, for being a person by yourself. I would avoid people who are psychopaths. They quite often come with a lot of charisma too. They're very impressive personalities. They kind of get into you very quickly and have what seem to be, apparently, easy answers. I also would advise beginning clients to try and find a group therapy situation. I feel that group pressure is often a much more effective and faster way to get people to change. I'm not saying that that client should change instantly, but I think that sometimes it's difficult for a therapist to get a person to change because then it changes the relationship and the therapist becomes the director, the authority figure, and the relationship may be destroyed. A group therapy situation may help a client check out his relationship with the therapist too."

*7. **Look for:*** "First and foremost, a human being of whatever gender that you just, in general, have a comfortable feeling talking to. If it has to be pushed after a month or two, there's just not a relationship. I would also suggest, very subjectively, that the therapist be a person of similar orientation and lifestyle. The therapist doesn't necessarily have to be woman if you're a woman, but if the therapist, for example, is culturally very different, there's enough room for misunderstanding and that just adds to it. I found my helpful therapist because I knew the kind of women who were seeing her. I would not look through a phone book, not through a hospital, but, if possible, I'd ask friends who are of the same kind of life style, because then you'll find someone who understands what your goals and needs are more readily. Someone who is very willing to discuss rather than arbitrate or to decide and judge. Someone, in short, who is accessible, who is open to opinions other than his own. I would suggest that the choice be not at all made on the basis of formal qualifications, as to what school the therapist is from, what degree he's achieved. Everyone will be to some degree trained, so that's a given. But, my therapist has spent the least number of years in school is what I'm saying. The degree of training over and above a minimum of qualifications and some kind of certification. I don't believe that because someone has gone that many more years to become a psychiatrist or a psychologist that this increases their qualifications. You will also generally pay a higher price for the increased amount of training. Believe it or not, I know people who judge therapists by what they charge. They say 'Oh, he charges ninety dollars an hour. He must be good.' Someone who is articulate. You have to respect their intelligence, their sensibilities, their perspectives, because your relationship is blown if you don't—not look up to them somehow—but feel as if you're dealing with someone who can very much put together what you're saying in a responsible and intelligent way and feed back whatever. Also—this is a key—that the therapist be accessible other than your one hour, which shows whether he's interested. That doesn't mean you're supposed to call him every night at nine o'clock. In summary, look for almost the same qualifications that you look for in a friend. Someone with whom you have some common interests. Someone who expresses himself to you and you can express yourself to him in a manner so you have common ground so that back and forth kind of expression can occur. Therapists are allowed to be irresponsible for as long as the general populace allows them to be so. People have to be far more responsible as to whom they are letting play with their minds and their emotions. You have to shop for a therapist just like you shop for anything else. If a medical doctor told you that you have to have open heart surgery tomorrow you would get other opinions. It is not quite an analogy, and I know that, but we in this culture have been used to being very much more sensitive to our physical health and not as much to our emotional health. A person is responsible to ask that therapist many questions. I asked my therapist 'What kinds of people do you see?' 'What are their life styles?' even though I kind of knew some of those answers before. Let them talk to you and judge whether or not you think you can be their friend. Because, although you're not bosom buddies, you are, in effect, becoming someone's friend. You are establishing a relationship that is going to be professional in nature. You're not going to go out to the movies together on Friday night more than likely, but therapists have traditionally held their clients at a distance, and if clients remain at that distance they will be held at that distance. And if you say 'No. No distance. Because this is my emotional health.' That's what I'm talking about in terms of friend."

8. Look for: "It's very important that therapists are not overly intellectual and that they help the client remain in touch with emotional qualities and not become overly involved with theoretical interpretations. This is something that is very difficult to tell in an initial interview. But, I would say that once a person decides on a therapist that they ought to have a number of sessions while they're still in a decision-making process about their choice before they make a final decision."

Avoid: "Consumers should avoid 'fad' therapies and should observe the therapist's behavior in relationship to his orientation. For example, there are therapists who consider themselves 'holistic' in their approach, dealing with the body and diet and so forth, but they move stiffly and smoke and there's a disparity between what they propose their orientation is and how they present themselves. And I think if there's an initial disparity of such a distressing magnitude to begin with that the client is immediately entering into a highly ambivalent situation and is dealing not just with his own problems but with the therapist's problems."

9. Look for: "The therapist's ability to allow the client to develop his own sense of values and to become what he is supposed to become. Which is one reason lovers or friends should never be therapists to each other, because there's always a hidden agenda. You really need someone who knows how to put his own values aside and allow you to develop yourself and be whoever you're supposed to be. The therapist should not be too serious. A therapist needs a good sense of humor. My helpful therapist is a riot. She just falls back in that chair and laughs. A therapist must have the ability to have intense feelings and to be able to handle them so the client can learn to develop feelings and control them. A therapist should be himself in a session and control himself also so the client might learn this. And I think a good therapist is one who breaks the rules. My helpful therapist and I went out. We had sessions in crazy places. I once went out to the beach with her to have a session at my summer house. We used a session to talk about my work or to read something. She let me meet her other patients, which in those days was against the rules. I met her husband. I talked with him. We had a session with him once when I was married. She let me take care of her in a sense. She let me drive her places. I really felt good about that. I liked to pick her up and take her places. I needed to feel that I was giving her something and she knew that. It was very hard to feel that I was just taking because I felt I was getting so much. And money had nothing to do with it. We hugged. I think in those days therapists didn't hug either. Those were the rules I broke with her. I think a good therapist has to have a variety of techniques. If you're a gestaltist but you see your client isn't doing well with it, then you cut it for a while and do something else. Or if a Freudian interpretation of dreams seems to be more valid you use that for a change. My helpful therapist was also growing, and I knew that. She was trying out new things. And I made fun of her. I think she's a lousy gestaltist. She said 'Be the rock.' I said 'You be the rock.' I didn't think it suited her, but I appreciated her willingness to try it. I think that therapists should be growing. They should also learn from the client. My helpful therapist learned from me too. If

I tried something and thought it was good she would ask me about it. So, I felt like a person. We had tremendous differences about religion, but she didn't ram her views of it down my throat. She tried to accept my views of it. If a therapist is not spiritual or religious and the client is they have to allow for that also. Again, it comes back to allowing the client to be whoever they're supposed to be. If I'm supposed to end up an orthodox rabbi, then he should get me to that place, whether or not he thinks that's a repulsive thing. And if he can't deal with it he should tell you 'What you want to be is good for you, but I can't handle it. I can't see how to get you there. So I'm bowing out'."

Avoid: "They get authoritarian. They think they know everything. You're a machine and they're going to fix you. Also, there's this crazy mystique among therapists that they can be off the wall but they can help anyone. I disagree with that. So, I think a client is not crazy when he wants to know what a therapist's life is like or what his values are. I know with politics clients do that. Or feminists try to see people who can help them be feminists. You have to be normal in a certain way to get a client to some kind of normal place in his life. I believe you have to break the rules, but you have to be in control of how you're going to break them. I remember telling my helpful therapist I had sexual fantasies about her and she said 'Don't worry because nothing's ever going to happen here.' And that made me feel very good. Now, with this jerk, he broke the rules too much by trying to seduce me. So, I never could really trust the man. I could trust that my helpful therapist would break the rules but there was still a limit. Avoid seeing someone who's overworked. I think therapy is an art and you have to be up for it. You can't give a client a good hour nine o'clock in the morning. Besides, a client thinks it's him. 'You're bored because I'm boring.' He forgets that you're bored because you're tired. Avoid a therapist who's too well-known because I think they get too cocky. They think 'I know all the answers.' My helpful therapist is famous, but she never did that. She's very humble in a certain way. She never really did it for a living when she started. She was very careful about who she would see, if they matched her. If she couldn't work with the person she sent him away. A lot of therapists will work with any client because they have to. And she wouldn't see that many people in a day so she could really give her clients a real hour. Like anything else. there's a good match. There's really a good therapist for you somewhere. And I think that therapists are different with different people too. If you don't like them they're not going to help you. I think it is good to find someone to have a really intense thing with, and I had that with her. You're playing out your life situation and you can see how you deal with the therapist and how you deal with other people in your life, if the therapist helps you use it that way. If he gets flattered and thinks he's wonderful or if it's scary for him and he can't handle it, then the client's going to be in bad shape. But if he uses it to show the client how he's doing the same thing out there in his other relationships, or how he doesn't have to do the same thing, or how it's a replay of his relationships with his parents, then it could be very, very helpful. When I asked questions she would answer me. And she'd say she's not feeling well if she wasn't. She'd try to be honest. Avoid someone who doesn't answer questions directly."

10. Look for: "I chose my helpful therapist because he was Jewish and because he would understand the plight of a 'Jewish princess.' Talk to prospective therapists and trust your instincts—how you feel, how you feel they relate to you. Are they listening or do they really hear what it is? Are they twisting things around so that you don't even understand it anymore? It's no different than if you're told you need an operation. You usually go for a second opinion. So why not treat your head like your body? It is a part of you."

11. Avoid: "The first thing that comes to mind—I keep thinking of the therapist who didn't help me—beware of therapists who don't smile."

12. Look for: "I believe in a definite first reaction chemistry kind of feeling, which is not necessarily right or wrong. But, I felt I was going to give it more than one session anyway. When I saw the helpful therapist, I liked him, and I went home and said 'Wow. I can't believe it. Someone's there to help me. Someone's really going to help me.' I was comforted, pacified, a soothing kind of feeling. Look for someone who you're not intimidated by, because if you can't be honest with someone you're not ever going to make any headway. I've heard people say

'How could you be really honest?' But there was no doubt that I was going to be completely honest. Even if there was nothing that related to me now, but happened in my past that I never wanted to say, I felt I wanted to have this openness, and I felt I could. If you feel you can't, then there's something missing. I think that's a tremendously important thing. Also, I felt he was very non-judgmental. He never said 'You're really okay. You can be attractive. You can be intelligent.' But, one time my feeling about myself as a woman was so poor [client's legs are paralyzed]. It was out of character for him, but he commented that someone in his office thought I was attractive and asked if he could have my phone number. It was not like him to say that but he said it because he knew it was something that I would like to hear. So, even with all that professionalism, he still did that."

13. Avoid: "That's a very individual question. It's very hard for me to tell someone what to avoid. Because you may feel worse before you feel better, and that doesn't mean that the therapist is bad. Too many people just stop therapy when that happens."

Author's note: Psychotherapy may be painful because confronting yourself and the realities of your life may be painful, and change is usually not easy. The client may experience this anxiety or discomfort or other distressing feelings regardless of who he has as a psychotherapist, or the therapist may cause or intensify these feelings with improperly used techniques, because of his noxious personality traits, or they may occur because of the nature of the relationship between the therapist and client. See discussion in this chapter about the fact that you don't have to suffer a lot to have effective psychotherapy. It is *not* true that the more or the longer you suffer the more successful your therapy will be.

14. Look for: "Somebody who's warm. The word loving may be too threatening. But I think in a gentle sort of way, like being warm and positive. Accepting is very basic. Not to have a set way of operating that stifles your own responses so you have to fit into his mold of how you should be. That's the whole problem of parental upbringing. If the therapist acts in that way he's just reinforcing that basic difficulty. We're all having to deal with the lack of acceptance of our being, and if the therapist has some model of how we should be, then that just doesn't work. As far as what therapists would do—there are gestaltists, there is psychodrama—the name is not of essential value so much as the degree of sensitivity and empathy. And also the therapist's willingness, openness to share himself can be helpful. And to not be afraid. If a therapist can deal with his own fears without being afraid. If he can deal with his own fears without being defensive."

Avoid: "Avoid somebody who has a strict model which he adheres to, or comes from an authoritarian position which will keep you stuck in being a child, basically being immature, and not allowing you to grow. And somebody who maintains a lot of 'shoulds.' That you should be functioning in a certain way. You should be changing a certain way to fit his expectations. Somebody who might be threatened if you question his way of operating. It's a tricky issue. On one hand, the therapist should be in charge, but at the same time the client should be allowed the freedom to question and to see just what's going on. Avoid someone who has a model that doesn't allow you to be yourself. Uptightness can be negative. And the therapist has to be able to meet the client at his level of being as opposed to a offering a head trip that's intellectual. It doesn't work when it's just an intellectual game. It's a meeting of the souls or hearts. It may sound romantic, but that's really what it comes down to. A loving relationship really heals."

15. Look for: "For me it's a feeling you have to go by. That you have some kind of rapport with the person. You have to trust your feelings to some extent. I guess because of the circumstances that I had with the unhelpful therapist, I would not recommend somebody who wants you to just lie on a couch. And I wouldn't recommend somebody who just says 'Um hm. Um hm.' I don't feel that would do any good. And I would suggest the kind of relationship that I have with the helpful therapist. Somebody who's open, who talks with you, and maybe the client might need somebody a little more directive. Some people do need direction sometimes."

Avoid: "If you've been with somebody for a period of time and you don't feel some kind of change, I would try to get out of it and find another one. If you don't feel change or better feelings about yourself or some insight, I would say to watch out for that. It's kind of a fine line to draw, but avoid somebody too directive who pushes you into something you don't really want to do."

16. Look for: "I think the most important thing is to find someone who will have a real feeling of professional commitment. This is hard to do because you don't know in the beginning who will be committed to your well-being and the relationship. And I'm not sure how you check that out. A lot of it will have to be after a few months. You have to truthfully think about what you're getting from an experience. And you should ask people to recommend therapists. You shouldn't just go to a therapist unless someone has recommended him to you. And then when you do go you should give it a trial period to see if something is happening, to see if you feel comfortable. You should feel comfortable. You should feel confident that the person will eventually help you. That should be conveyed to you. You should feel that the therapist treats you in a very humanistic way. And I think he should be open to evaluating with you the effects of the therapy at all different points in the therapy. He should be open to hearing your criticism of the therapy and your directives about where it should be going. You should have a sense that the person is going to stick with you and that if they don't like what you're saying they're not going to end your therapy. That a professional commitment is to continue with the person no matter what's being said in the office. That he's not going to pull something outrageous like one day raise your fee so high that you can't pay it. That he's going to be on time for your appointment. And he's not going to change your appointment time or tell you he's going to be late. All those things indicate that someone takes his job seriously. And he should also be open to suggestions on how to help you. A therapist shouldn't have an agenda before you get in there. He should help you to find what your agenda is, who you want to be. And then work with you on that. He shouldn't impose his values on you."

Avoid: "The first thing that comes to mind is a therapist who recommends that you see him more often than you feel you can afford or more often than you want to because he tells you that you're too sick, so sick you need it. I don't subscribe to that. And I think it's deceitful. I think that relatively healthy clients should decide how often they want therapy. I think you have to avoid someone you're not comfortable with. Avoid therapists who are attacking and destructive. Avoid therapists who offer interpretations of your behavior that don't make sense to you. Avoid therapists who cancel appointments and change appointments around and don't give notice of vacations and raised fees. That's definitely to be avoided. And people who have a set agenda for their clients. And then I think that after a while if you feel that you're not getting anything out of therapy, you should be wary of a therapist who tried to keep you in therapy when you're expressing doubts about it."

17. Look for: "After an experience in therapy a client might say 'That was a really powerful experience, but what the [censored] does that have to do with my life?' Or 'What was that all about?' For example, if the Freudian analyst pressed and delved into my childhood and my relationships with my parents as a child constantly so that I understood that, I might say 'That's all very interesting, but what relevance does that have to my life right now?' You may understand that there's an immediate problem, and that in the back of all that, and obviously this reflects a psychoanalytic orientation, that the reason it happened to become a problem in the first place may go back to the time you were five years old. But it has to have some relationship to what's going on in your life now. I think that people go into therapy because there's something the matter with them and they want to work on what's the matter with them. And if there's nothing pressing the matter with them and they just simply want to understand themselves better, they can focus on different kinds of things. But, if there's something that doesn't really relate to or begin to solve what it is that's the matter with their lives that takes them into therapy, then that may not be real effective therapy. If a person is drinking, alcoholically, and is dealing in therapy with conflicts with his mother when he was four or five years old, I'm not sure that that's really relevant to the immediate problem or what's the matter with his life right now. Do you feel good about the therapist? Do you feel you can trust him? You can use a lot of your *thinking* skills, but you basically have to ask 'Does this *feel* right?' Is he a person of substance, integrity, his own person, his own man? And that I could not manipulate him.

And yet he wouldn't kick me out or he wouldn't reject me for trying to manipulate him. He would be able to call me on it and to have an honest adult conversation about it. A good therapist has a sensitivity. And I don't know how well that can be trained into a person. It's just something you feel from a therapist. Anxiety is an integral part of therapy. I was anxious a lot, but it was just enough to make things come to the surface without being unbearable. The other extreme would have been for the level of anxiety to be so bearable that it would be just too comfortable for me. I don't know how you can look for that, how you can find that. If by the first or second session you feel challenged without feeling threatened, I guess that's the best way to say it. If a therapist questions whether the way you're presenting your life to him is in your best interest, a good therapist will give you the hope that there may be an alternative, but not judgmentally condemn or criticize you, and not say 'You have to stop doing that. You have to give that up right away. You have to stop being what you are.' That would be threatening for a client. People are what they are for a reason. And it may not be the most productive or effective way to live his life and the client may want to change those things, but if he chooses to give up the things he is he has to do it gradually and at a pace that's comfortable. And if that pace becomes slowed down and he needs a gentle kick in the ass from the therapist, that's exactly what he has to get without someone standing in back of him with a whip. Look for a therapist who has a sense of hope and optimism. And a person who can help you realize that potential."

Avoid: "Someone who makes a client uncomfortable, *real* uncomfortable. A certain amount of discomfort is to be expected, but avoid *real* discomfort. Because when the bottom line comes down, if it feels right to you, it's your life and your feelings are right for you. If you say to yourself 'There's something wrong here. I don't know what it is. I don't know why it is. I don't even know what's telling me there's something wrong. But there's something wrong here.' Trust that."

18. Look for: "It's very difficult. Recommendations may or may not be helpful, because it depends upon where the person who's recommending you is at. I think you have to be lucky. I think that if you're a consumer and you don't know much about psychotherapy and you've had very little experience, I think that it's like buying a car, which is blind. I would say that before you make a commitment you really have to do a lot of shopping. I would look for somebody who could be open about himself. Not that he should tell you about his life history. But, somebody who could, at least, tell you what his philosophy is or where he's going, and about his concept of treatment so you at least know what you're buying. Ask him to tell you what he thinks are your problems, and tell him what you think are your problems. For example, I came in with a problem. I was unable to have a satisfying relationship with a man. But that really turned out to be the least of the problems. That was just a symptom of a variety of a whole set of complex things. Such as I really needed a dependency on my original family more than I wanted anything else. Whether or not I had it or didn't have it or had it in fantasy and not reality was not really most significant. I really didn't want to leave home. What does the therapist see as a goal in five years or two years or six months?"

Avoid: "Everyone needs different kinds of things. The good psychotherapist I was with would be horrible for a variety of different clients. I think that if a client were going to see him primarily for support from him, he wouldn't get it. If a client wanted to have someone hold his hand, he wouldn't get it. My good therapist is not into holding a client's hand or helping him through a particular crisis. He's not into feeling sorry or empathizing what a terrible lot in life you have. He's not a terribly nurturing person. My unhelpful therapist was very dependency-enhancing. He certainly was into feeding dependency and bringing out how terrible things were. That didn't help me and I didn't want my helpful therapist to do that. I would avoid somebody who is rigid in any sense, moralistic, punitive, who only sees one way of doing something, who's going to promise anything. I would never see somebody who is not open about himself. I don't mean that he would tell me he has three kids, but someone who lets me know that he has the knowledge, that he has also experienced the kind of thing that I've experienced on some level, and he knows what the problem is. I would never see someone who hasn't been in psychotherapy as a client himself.

And not because it was part of his required professional training. Absolutely never. I would want to see someone who could admit to having had his own crises and who has been reasonably successful in working them through. I would stay away from somebody I thought was cold."

19. Avoid: "I had one meeting with a gentleman when I was seeking help who was very solicitous. And I was in tears and very unhappy and he proceeded to pat and pat and pat and he proceeded to pat on parts of my anatomy that I don't think really required much sympathy. I think there is a certain amount of faith and trust you put into your professionals. And, unfortunately, it is only when you discover that the doctor has sewn your appendix to your tonsils that you realize that this may not be the greatest doctor in the world. Or if you find that you are getting radio signals in your teeth, you may decide he's not the greatest dentist. And with a psychotherapist I'm afraid that the damage is even harder to detect. This is one field where self-policing is very, very required."

CHAPTER 2

How Do Psychotherapists Help?

In this chapter consumers tell you *how* they feel their psychotherapists helped them change, what the therapists *did,* how the helpful therapist was different from the therapist who didn't help or even harmed, and how their lives changed.

1. "He helped me with his interest and concern. I felt I wasn't alone. The initial difference is not insight or interpreting defenses, but not being alone. During your first session, when you're describing your plight, if you feel you're not alone, that there's someone with his hand on your shoulder. That's the first thing. After that experience, I was able to hear him. After I felt a hand on my shoulder. And he helped me with his insights and creativity and artist's mind. He puts things in a metaphorical way, doesn't stick to a structured, rigid perspective. It's a humanistic experience. And I can hear things

much better with his humor. Humor is important. The other thing is his high regard for me."

2. "He was able to interact. If you can't interact and you can't relate, then not only aren't you a therapist, but you're not a human being. I just can't see this behind the couch stuff. He listened to what the problems were. He tried to get some kind of understanding of what was going on. He tried to see where I was in the situation and what was real in the situation and what was my own fantasy and what was stuff that I was neurotically bringing to it and to try and sift that out. To reflect back where my interaction was neurotic and where it was valid. Where it was reality-based. He reflected back what his feelings were and his interpretation was about what was real and what was neurotic, and then I was able to take his interpretation and insight and work with it myself so that I had a different kind of insight, a different kind of viewing of the whole situation and where I fit in the situation. The therapist who didn't help was terribly distant and somehow mystical. I took his not relating as being a kind of mystical, god-like quality, that somehow he was doing something that I in my ignorance could not understand, and it was something that was totally my own problem. Not only was I not functioning the way I fantasized that I should be functioning, but I couldn't even understand my therapist, what he was doing. My helpful therapist helped in terms of giving a more real picture of what a therapist should be, what a man should be. He was able to be a human being. I could see him as

a human being and relate to him as a human being, rather than this some strange non-understandable being. My reaction to that was that not only did I come in not feeling well, but I was worse, because I went away feeling 'My God, I'm really terrible. I'm really sick. Because I can't even understand, I can't even function with my therapist.' The therapist is supposed to be the person you function with. He's supposed to understand you. And the fact that there wasn't any communication going on, there wasn't any relating or interacting, made it worse. Because the expectation was that it should be. It wasn't just like you meet somebody on the street and the person doesn't talk to you and you don't hit it off with that person. It wasn't this kind of a chance interaction. Here was a specific relationship which was supposed to have communication, was supposed to help me grow. And none of that was happening. And he was still the expert and that made me just completely ill, that I could not relate to him."

3. "She loved me. She let me love her. I loved her so much. She accepted my extreme sides. She got me to accept myself. She gave me objective ways of seeing I was getting better. I remember when she told me my handwriting changed. She helped me develop my center. She told me I was talented. I didn't really understand that. And I began to believe it and use it. I think I got in touch with my own unconventionality. That's my way-of-being and that's the way I am in the world and that's okay. I didn't have to be like anybody. I could be myself.

She also was very involved in my projects. She would help. Once I had to write this horrible lesson plan and I was screaming 'I can't do it.' She said 'I'll help you do it. I'll look at it.' Sure enough, she was right. I used it for years. She saw me as a person outside of the office at times. I felt very good about that. She wasn't ashamed of me because I was a 'nut.' In fact, she was very proud of me."

4. "She helped with very specific kinds of hard facts that she would research. The therapist who didn't help me never did anything along those lines. For example, she helped me get a job by researching centers that market people, got names and telephone numbers for me. She also served as my one anchor at a very chaotic time in my life when I didn't even have an apartment and my whole life was upheaved. And she very much pointed out that 'This is something that's consistent. You are here Wednesday at five o'clock. Use this as something stable in your life right now,' and it helped. Sometimes when I couldn't get a handle on things it would be something for me to know that was going to be there. That providing of consistency was enormously helpful, securing. She provided me with feedback, with various perspectives that I had not seen before, with a sort of role playing. If I had an imminent confrontation with someone, we would go through it. She provided me with a great sense that this was someone whose opinion I could really respect in terms of being bright, intuitive, communicative, articulate, and objective. She provided me with just knowing that that was there. That was quite directly

related to my being able to do a lot. Clients have friends and mates and people to talk to, but she provided herself in the emotionally comforting role of a confidant, and also in a very professional and adequate role. Someone who will really give me a responsible answer and help to direct me without really pushing me down a particular path. And she tied a lot of things together. She might say to me 'You're talking about this and that now. It really strikes me that that has a whole lot to do with the discussion we had about such and such last month,' and it really made sense. And she provided something that no other therapist has. She holds sessions in her home. She has let it be known, obviously not to be abused, but she is available any time day or night. When she is on vacation she will let her service know where she is and she calls back. She'll see me on Sunday if she can. And she had me see medical doctors to see if there is something physically wrong with me, with glands or hormones. And everyone thinks that something is wrong. But, she makes clear that she feels that I have certain emotional difficulties above and beyond the possible medical problems."

5. "You wouldn't have known me then from the way I am now. I wasn't talking to anybody. He more or less drew me out and gave me an example that people weren't all bad. And I was able to get things that had been on my mind for a long time articulated. I have good verbal ability but that was blocked up. He freed it up. I was frozen inside and scared to move. He encouraged me to get out of my shell

and coerced me. He used a variety of approaches—encouragement and coercion, talking about the weather and how it makes me feel, small talk, in depth analysis of my childhood, or analysis of my dreams. When I first started with him I had trouble keeping my appointments and he told me that he couldn't see me anymore if I didn't keep my appointments with him. In that way he was kind of firm. Which meant he was serious about me, interested in me. He saw me with my parents several times and got me into a boarding house. I think the primary thing he did was to define some of my problems and orient me toward looking at myself in a conceptual manner, trying to organize what I was doing and why I was doing it. He was flexible. Sometimes we'd talk about dreams I had, other times how I felt at my job, and things like philosophy and psychology. He also gave me leeway, a certain freedom to control what was going on in the therapy session. He wasn't after me on one point continuously. The therapist who didn't help me was existential and had one philosophical mode in his therapy, and he would always hit on the same points all the time."

6. "All I really needed was somebody to help me find the right way to get the independence from my parents that I needed. All I needed was somebody to guide me. Just somebody I could talk to. She told me 'Maybe you're a little bit too involved with your parents.' I would think about that a little bit and I would try not to let things bother me so much with them, get involved so much with them.

That helped me a little bit. She really helped, but somehow I would go back into the same pattern. That's why I had to go to her so much. Every week she'd help me or else I'd slip back. I needed constant talking to. Also, when I was jealous of my sisters, she tried to let me know that I was just as good as them. I thought they were better because they were so thin and pretty and I was very fat. And I was very self-conscious and I felt like I was the center of attraction and everyone was laughing at me all the time. She said I'm not an ugly person and I should try to lose some weight and I shouldn't be jealous of my sisters."

7. "He believed in me. That's it, completely. That summarizes it. He believed in me. He believed I was a worthwhile person. He believed in my potential and never for one minute did he vacillate from conveying to me that belief that I was a valuable, worthwhile, important person. There was never a single time that I saw him that I did not feel that at least during that hour I was the most important person to him. For that hour of his life and my life I was the most important person in the world to him, because that was my hour. I knew that there were other people before me and after me and I knew other people who were in therapy with him, but I never had the feeling that he was preoccupied, that he was bored, that he was disinterested, that he was anything other than totally interested in me. And I never believed for a minute that he believed any of my self-doubts. I knew he just believed in my potential, in my ability, and all the positive things about

me. And through his believing in those things and because I thought so much of him, I ultimately came to believe in them."

8. "He was for me the most supportive person I've ever know, outside of my wife. He never told me I was wrong. I suppose it's his way of asking a question, or his total flexibility. It was sometimes very difficult for me to let go enough to feel secure in what was going on. About a year and a half ago I really felt that things had to change between him and me. One of the reasons I wanted to change was that I graduated with a M.S. in guidance and counseling. The whole program is clinically oriented so while I was in therapy with him I was getting information about techniques that I had never really been exposed to before. Every once in a while something would happen and it would come into my head that 'That's a technique. I wonder if that's real.' So, once I talked about that and he said 'Well, ask and I'll tell you if it is.' So, we did that for a while and in a couple of months I said I really wanted some direct feedback. I didn't want Rogerian answers [techniques of Carl Rogers]. I didn't want 'So, you don't feel well today.' If I ask you, I want an answer back. I think I know enough to either accept or reject it. And we did that for a while and we still do it. I wanted to check out certain things that I wasn't sure about, that I really didn't feel very secure about. He's even given me the security to disagree with him. Because of his flexibility, because he was willing to do anything, I could play around with a lot of things to see what fit. I also had a feeling that

while I was learning something it was not like taking castor oil. With the therapist who didn't help me, it didn't taste very good. It may be beneficial but it didn't taste very good."

9. "His presence helped. When I go to therapy, what I go for is to throw out information. It's kind of like baseball in a way. You pitch and you bat. And I throw it out and I hear it come back to me. I needed to hear these things come back to me. Just because it was a thought, I didn't know how valid some of these thoughts were until I threw them out and heard them."

10. "My father was not available to me as a child and was not there to be supportive of me and had no interest in my work as an artist, or if he did have an interest, his anxiety about it was so high because of now knowing anything about art that he never expressed interest. My helpful therapist attended my openings, my one man shows, occasionally came to my studio to see my work, and worked with me with the symbols that occurred in the work as a vehicle for interpreting behavior and understanding of self. So, his stepping out of his role as therapist, at least what I thought was the role of a therapist, was very gratifying in giving me some of the things that I hadn't received from my father. And since I saw him as a very respectable and likeable person, it was easy for me to identify with him and to feel that I wanted to be like him and to experience the support as extremely valuable in the treatment. When I asked the first therapist, the one who didn't help me, about coming to see my work or

when I expressed concern about not ever touching, not ever hugging after an emotional situation, when I expressed a desire for anything that seemed outside of the limitations, she was very emphatic about defining what the limitations were and how the limitations were a function of the treatment. So, the treatment was experienced as being very non-gratifying, even though it was provocative and intellectually stimulating and challenging. It was not gratifying. So, my helpful therapist gratified me a lot as well as confronted me when necessary. He gratified me with his ability to be human and to respond in a human way when I needed that response. Quite frankly, I don't think that he did it as a therapeutic technique. I think he did it out of his humanness and out of his genuine interest. And I'm sure that with some clients he is more comfortable doing that than with others. His ability to do that may have something to do with his experiences too. He may have been in a place where his experience as a therapist had given him the security and the comfort to be able to step out of the boundaries more easily. But, I'm sure it was orientation as well as personality."

11. "He wasn't threatening, wasn't overwhelming, was accepting, empathic, he was basically there for me, was very supportive, open to hearing whatever I had to say, gave me unconditional positive regard. He did offer some of his insights, but his insights didn't really change me. It was more like the acceptance and his being as opposed to the things he said. More the way he presented himself

than any information that he shared with me."

12. "Initially I think it was showing me that it was okay to feel depressed, okay to feel sorry for myself, it's okay to feel all these negative things. And, by feeling them, you're more in touch with them, not constantly trying to hide them. There was a point when he said about my physical thing [client's legs are paralyzed] 'That's the way it is. If you can't change something you have to accept what it is.' And I felt anger. But I was so comfortable with him that I was able to say 'I was angry with you. You don't know what it's like.' But, again, it sunk in and I know that he was right. I can even relate it to other people who are in situations that can't be changed. It's not physical, but it's other things. And he always had a little game to play and it always sounded off the wall when he'd tell me. Like as far as feeling that people are staring at me, he would say 'Well, instead of focusing on the people who are staring at you, it may not work, but it works for some people, say to yourself 'I'm going to be really angry at anyone who doesn't look at me. I want everyone to look at me.' And I thought that sounded so dumb and I laughed at him. And I found myself doing that in a kidding way. In other words, I was focusing on the people who weren't. And there were so many little things that he would do that changed my behavior. I'm very anxious and I anticipate. Next week at so and so time I have to do this and I'd be crazy now. But take each hour as it comes. It was again simply him verbalizing what I should do. Say to yourself 'Today's going to be a

bad day' or 'Today I'm going to make five mistakes.' It was like a list and I would always kind of laugh about them to myself, but I would always end up using them, and it always seemed to work. It was strange. And that was the interaction that helped me. With the therapist who didn't help me there was never any kind of 'How can I help you'?"

13. "He taught me some behavioral techniques. But, mainly I think it was his value of me as a person. I valued me as a person and most of the people in my family valued me as a person, but I think I needed to really talk about that as an issue, and I think that if I were to say that he helped me in any one constructive really big way, that would be the way. He really lets me know that he values me as a person. I have important things to say. And he's willing to take the trip with me. To hear me out and to be part of my life during those sessions that I see him. And sort of get into my skin a little bit and find out what's going on and how to work it out. And he's very open. Sometimes I'll say to him 'Look, I see something's going on with you. What are you thinking?' He'll be honest and he'll say 'I'm not sure, but I'll let you know in a couple of minutes' and then he will."

14. "He listened to what I said, encouraged those things that were good, saw things that were good that I never saw. And he was pretty consistent. No double messages which I find often come from people."

15. "She was more understanding. More sym-

pathetic. And the way she went about talking to me. And she listens to me. The unhelpful therapist never listened to me. I'd come in, I'd sit down, she'd ramble on. And when I expressed myself, how I felt, I don't think she was really listening. The helpful therapist listens to me and hears what I'm saying. And she's more sympathetic. She's with me."

16. "He didn't let me feel sorry for myself. He wasn't into feeling sorry or pity or bemoaning my fate. But, on the other hand, he was very supportive of growth. He was very supportive of my dates with men. He was very supportive of pain. He felt that pain in some way was ennobling. Not that it should be in and of itself, but it was certainly nothing to be ashamed of. And he felt that conflict was positive, and that it was better to be in conflict than not to be in conflict. And it was better to have anxiety than not to have anxiety. That at least with anxiety and conflict there was an attempt toward growth. And although it was painful and one would feel better in the very short run if one didn't have anxiety, that if one didn't have that one was dead. And what he basically did was to respect the process of growth. The unhelpful therapist would only feed growth under his conditions. Growth could only take place according to his schedule. And his major aim was not growth, but dependency. It was growth through dependency, by dependency."

17. "He allowed me through a very subtle evolutionary process to live my life from day to day as I saw it should be lived and deal with the results thereof. He never suggested, advised, told, ad-

monished, complimented. I didn't get slapped down or patted. Maybe he'd be different with someone else, but he saw what my needs were. It was a very fine gradual needlepoint weaving. The therapist who didn't help me was very much the opposite on all these points. I didn't want that again."

18. "I'm going to give most of the credit to myself. The helpful therapist's method allowed me to see things. She gave me the space, I guess. Because she was softer, laid back, as opposed to the unhelpful therapist, she allowed me the space that I needed to bring in my issues, to recognize them internally."

19. "First of all there was the human being, interchange with a human being. It's kind of like nurturing a flower, nurturing a plant. I felt that I began to develop as a person. The human parts began to come out. I began to relate a lot better, relate with a lot more depth. This has taken a long time. How she started to do that was to turn me on to different things and to turn me in different directions. For instance, I really was interested in food and cooking, so she really encouraged that a tremendous lot. I was able to go along with that very easily and explore those things and feel, just look at the things I produced. It was in that way that I began to grow much more. Other sensory things too. My friendships. Other people began to be important. A sense of knowing people, of valuing people, of there being give and take between people. As this process went on feelings began to flow much more. A sense

of joy, really, I guess, even though I was very depressed through a lot of this time. She was able to reduce a huge load of guilt that I was carrying around that I constantly aroused in myself and a very punitive sense of the 'should bes.' She was able to reassure that part of me, to kind of put those things to rest. They were put into a context so that quite often what I did was focus on my anxieties and they became enlarged and took over. So, they would be put back into a context so that they weren't so overwhelming. Also, my feelings, especially my anger, tend to take over a lot of the time, so I think we had to work on that a lot. She's helped me to make limits and set limits in terms of where my emotions go, how far they go, and in terms of what I'm doing to other people, myself, and my environment."

20. "Mostly, I think, she gave me the time to change. And that meant a very long term investment. And for me that was very important, that I had the sense from her that our relationship could go on for a number of years. And out of that relationship would come, there have come, the gains I've made. So, I feel, mostly, it's the involvement of saying 'Well, it may take years to accomplish what we want to accomplish.' Sticking with it, not pushing for it to go faster. Being genuinely interested in me and what I want and not pushing me in a way that she would want, so I could find out what I am. And that's through talking. I think people change through talking with someone who really wants to hear what they have to say. I think that's how she

did it. I think she's very skillful. And she's a trained psychotherapist. Of course, that never hurts."

21. "With the fact that there has to be a certain acceptance. That the world does not accommodate. That things are the way they are. That you must, to a degree, have a certain acceptance of things you cannot change. You cannot move the world. He more or less made me secure enough in myself to accept the things that were upsetting."

22. "He used the Socratic method wherein I answered my own questions. If he asked me to free associate the obvious thing would be what happened on the way down to see him, for instance, or if I walked in kind of agitated he would say 'You look a little upset this morning. What's the problem? What's bothering you?' Maybe I would tell him 'There was a traffic jam and it took me a long time to get here.' And he would ask questions and I would answer them and in my answering the questions or in answering my own questions I came to realize that the anger was really not the traffic jam. There were things that went beyond it. It was a free association kind of thing. I arrived at my own answers with his help, rather than him telling me what happened and what didn't happen and what should have happened and what I should have done and why I did what I did. The other therapist, the one who didn't help me, would have said something to the effect 'Now isn't that ridiculous. What are you getting so angry about?' which would have been true but it would have aroused an anger toward him in me to his kind of being critical, telling me what

to do, and it just was not conducive to getting anything deeper and beyond the specific anger at that particular incident."

23. "I can give an example. I once described a situation to the non-helpful therapist where I was driving in traffic and I was late for an appointment and I got caught by traffic lights and I was very angry. And the first therapist, the one who didn't help me, was sympathetic. He said 'Oh, yes. It's happened to me, too. Sometimes those things happen.' And he let it go at that. It came up again, the same anecdote, with the helpful therapist. He listened to the story without interrupting. And then at the end said 'Let's get into what you were feeling when the traffic light turned red against you. Did you think at the time it did that it was directed at you particularly? That it was there to impede your progress?' Of course, it was a question that made me a little irritable when he asked it because it was kind of a rhetorical question. I could see that after the session was over, the reason he asked it was that it was foolish for me to feel anger at the time because traffic lights are random occurrences. And in talking about it I got to understand some of the unrealistic anger that I used to feel and still do from time to time, but, of course, much less often though. So, just in that one little story, I'm trying to explain it, he seemed more concisive and more able to develop a seemingly innocent story and not treat even trivial occurrences as unimportant."

CHAPTER 3

Psychotherapy Can Be Harmful

Can psychotherapy actually be harmful? Psychologist Allen E. Bergin, Director of the Institute for Studies in Values and Human Behavior at Brigham Young University, and co-editor with Sol Garfield of the *Handbook of Psychotherapy and Behavior Change,* a standard reference used by researchers of psychotherapy, says that some clients are worse after psychotherapy, referring to this as the "deterioration effect." He and only a few others have written about qualities of psychotherapists that can *cause* their clients to be worse instead of better.

Writing in popular magazine *Psychology Today* in November 1975 on the topic "Psychotherapy can be dangerous," he says:

> "Suppose every psychotherapist had a sign over his door that read: 'Psychotherapy may be harm-

> ful to your mental health.' That might not stop everyone, but it would make many people more careful, which wouldn't be a bad idea. . . . Evidence from empirical studies and personal reports from former patients indicates that some psychotherapists, like some drugs, should be banned, and that some forms of therapy should be dispensed only under the most careful controls."

He quotes Michael Scriven, a member of the American Psychological Association's Board of Social and Ethical Responsibility, as having questioned "the moral justification for dispensing psychotherapy, given the state of studies which would lead the Food and Drug Administration to ban its sale if it were a drug." "Unfortunately," says Dr. Bergin:

> "there is no equivalent of a Food and Drug Administration to monitor therapies and therapists for effectiveness. There is no psychological FDA to root out unproved claims or dangerous practices. University selection procedures, professional societies, and state-licensing laws help, but they don't exert much control over the therapist's personality and technique. Until they do, let the buyer beware."

Hans Strupp, Distinguished Professor of Psychology, Vanderbilt University, and co-author of the book *Psychotherapy for Better or Worse: The Problem of Negative Effects*, researches what he calls "negative effects" in psychotherapy. He and Bergin have been the major researchers and writers on the subject of harmful psychotherapy. He says that therapists may see personality problems in others, but may not see them in themselves. He and his co-authors say that some of these possible "noxious personality traits" are: ignorance, exploitiveness, coldness, obsessional analyzing, excessive need to make people change, excessive unconscious hostility, seductiveness, lack of interest or warmth, neglect, pessimism, sadism, absence of genuineness, greed, narcissism, lack of self-understanding. Strupp says that harm can be the result of the therapist's errors in diagnosis or misapplications or deficiencies of technique.

It is not psychotherapy, the process, that is harmful. Rather, it is the people who do psychotherapy, the psychotherapists, who as Strupp writes are "practitioners who somehow failed to do justice to their craft."

I must clarify here that the therapist's personality or his technical skills are *not* the only possible cause of unsuccessful or ineffective psychotherapy. Some clients would get worse with any therapist as well as without a therapist. We don't know enough yet about what makes people distressed or how to help everyone. But, some psychotherapists do harm their clients by using improper technical skills, or just by being who they are.

Most schools granting degrees in psychology use numerical grades on tests of mathematical and verbal abilities to choose those who will become psychologists working as psychotherapists. Schools training social workers, psychiatrists, and others who become psychotherapists don't do much better in choosing their students. They do not screen out prospective students who have emotional difficulties which are likely to interfere with their work with clients. A healthy personality, being able to get along well with other people, and knowing and being able to understand and use techniques of psychotherapy are what a therapist needs to be able to help.

I remember one of my co-workers, a psychologist, who thought that all of her clients were angry and needed to "get it out." Actually, she was angry herself, but she denied it, was not aware of her own anger, and she thought others were angry instead. In fact, she denied so much in her life that all through the months she was dying from cancer when I visited her at home she would tell me she'd see me back at work in a few days, not acknowledging the fact that she was dying. Another psychologist I know acts out an image of what he wants to be rather than being the person he is. He is pompous and arrogant and unaware and pretends to know what he doesn't know. And his clients feel misunderstood and don't feel cared for. In fact, he is unable to care or to have many authentic feelings. A psychiatrist I used to work with gave the same diagnosis to nearly all of his clients, and he didn't know that he was describing himself, not his clients. Another psychiatrist walks down the street and diagnoses people. He knows someone for 30 seconds and he tells me "That man is obviously paranoid schizophrenic." And he doesn't keep confidences. He talks about his clients.

When psychotherapy is not successful, very often clients blame themselves. Quite often therapists blame their clients also for failures, with variations of the explanation "He's not amenable to treatment," meaning that the client is unable to benefit from therapy. When the client also blames himself, the client is truly the victim.

I recall a very funny comment by psychologist Harold Greenwald, Founder and Director of the Direct Decision Therapy Institute in San Diego, California, President of the Division of Humanistic Psychology of the American Psychological Association, author of several books, and co-author of *The Happy Person,* in which he intended to point out the arrogance of many therapists and the common alliance that they use to protect themselves from responsibility for unsuccessful therapy by blaming the client for failures. He said "It's great being a psychologist. I never have failures, only resistant patients."

Consumers can find out more about the qualifications of plumbers than psychiatrists, psychologists, and psychiatric social workers concludes a report titled "Through the Mental Health Maze: A Consumer's Guide to Finding a Psychotherapist, Including a Sample Consumer/Therapist Contract," by Sallie Adams and Michael, Orgel, which is available from an organization founded by Ralph Nader: Public Citizen, Health Research Group, 2000 P Street NW, Washington, D.C. 20036. In 1975 the

Nader group sent questionnaires to Washington, D.C. area psychiatrists, psychologists, and psychiatric social workers, attempting to collect information to be used in a consumer directory so consumers might be able to learn about the differences among these health care providers, because they contended "the health professions are, for all practical purposes, unregulated as to the quality of the services they render or the prices they charge," and there are great differences among practitioners in the professions of psychiatry, psychology, and psychiatric social work, and even among individual practitioners within the same professions. Of the 706 questionnaires mailed to psychiatrists with clinical practices, 172 were completed and returned. Psychologists completed and returned 166 of 914 sent, and psychiatric social workers had the best percentage with 110 of 331 sent, nearly a third. The Washington Psychiatric Society members were especially protective of their privacy with the President-Elect (because the President was on vacation) responding by sending a letter to members of the society to "recommend caution to our members in responding." He writes that the Society's Council "suggests that not returning the questionnaire would be the preferred action." The reason for this fear of answering simply factual, non-intrusive questions about their training, office hours, fees charged, kind of therapy practiced, types of medication used, and other aspects of the ways they work with their clients is "It appears to Council that there are many defects in this questionnaire and that the possibilities for unfavorable slanting of the material are considerable. Conscientious answers to it may be construed against the responder and dishonest answers in his favor." This just simply is not true. This questionnaire is available from Nader's group if you want to judge it for yourself. If the clients of these psychiatrists were so self-protective that they wouldn't answer such questions if asked by the psychiatrists, the diagnosis might be "guarded," "suspicious," and even "paranoid."

Sidney M. Wolfe, a physician with Nader's group, writes in the introduction to the report of the survey:

> "With few exceptions, the process of collecting the data for these directories has been met with an extraordinary amount of resistance from the local or state... societies. It is as though these trade associations feel obligated to resist any efforts to crack the veneer of uniformity they give to the public about their members—namely the assumption that anyone who is licensed to practice... is as good for all purposes as anyone else. This attitude is most clearly seen when consumers call the local society for the names of [psychotherapists] they can go to. The consumer is likely to be given the name of anyone licensed in a manner not unlike Russian Roulette."

The report goes on:

> "Much more so than with either the doctor or dentist directories [also created by this group] we received dozens of unusual calls—especially from psychiatrists—objecting to this directory.

> One particularly upset psychiatrist caller charged 'You must be out of touch with reality to compile such a directory.' Others asked 'What is really behind these questions?'"

The first comment about reality contact is an attempt by this psychiatrist to discredit those creating the directory by diagnosing them as "mentally ill." The second comment about the real intent of the questions is definitely suspicious and defensive. What does this caller have to hide from the public?

What does Nader's group suggest you do about protecting yourself when you begin psychotherapy? Just what you might expect from attorney Ralph Nader, is a legal written contract between you and your therapist. A contract cannot guarantee you helpful therapy, but it is an attempt to define the nature of services—what your therapist agrees to do for you. It's a way to invade the privacy of the therapist's office. It's a way to negotiate as an equal party and to hold him accountable for at least some of his behavior. It's also a way to demystify therapy and to avoid months or years of needless "therapy" by defining problems and setting goals periodically and evaluating progress toward those goals.

What can you do to prevent being harmed? The Ralph Nader group recommends:

> "If you have doubts, complaints, or dissatisfaction concerning a therapist, the course of treatment or anything else, discuss it with [him.] If you are angry, tell [him]. If the differences cannot be ironed out between the two of you . . . then

you are faced with the choice of getting another opinion or terminating therapy. A therapist should not be insulted if you ask for a consultation [opinion from another therapist], especially if the therapy has been going on for a long time or if the two of you differ over what the best goals are for you. Seeking another opinion is not an irrevocable step away from your therapist; indeed, the therapist may benefit from the insights provided by another [therapist] as much as you may."

Psychotherapists, generally, are unwilling to give their customers information. They also usually do not publicly discuss, write about, or adequately attempt to prevent harm to clients. Bergin says that "horror stories . . . are often shared privately among clients and professionals but are rarely published." They are published in this book.

E. Fuller Torrey clinical and research psychiatrist in Washington, D.C., who for four years was Special Assistant to the Director of the National Institute of Mental Health, has been a contributing editor to popular magazine Psychology Today, has been nominated for a National Book Critics Circle award, and is author of *Witchdoctors and Psychiatrists*, believes that "The best defense against incompetence in this field is an educated consumer." Consumers are beginning to write about their experiences. They're beginning to educate themselves. The *Consumer Health and Nutrition Index* summarizes articles from popular magazines, newsletters, and books, and categorizes them according to subject, including the topic of psychotherapy. My favorite titles from the past two years are "Pick a Therapist. Years and Years on the Wrong Couch," and "Shrunk by Your Shrink? Should you Keep Your Therapist?"

And the August 3l, 1987, cover story of *New York* Magazine is "Prisoners of Psychotherapy," by Terri Minsky, about therapists who discourage their clients from ending therapy. The client's ultimate goal in psychotherapy is termination, that is after it is successful. Ideally, the ultimate satisfaction in a therapist's work should be when a client is at a good point emotionally, is reasonably independent and autonomous, and leaves the therapist.

An example of what actually might happen is the scenario given as this article continues. After five years, therapy sessions for Elizabeth "passed pleasantly," and were "mostly idle chitchat. It was clearly time to quit therapy. But when Elizabeth broached the idea with her therapist, he would bring up some niggling trouble, usually with her mother, a subject that was always good for 45 minutes of discussion." Elizabeth would leave thinking "Okay, next week we'll finish." This went on for six months. She knew her therapist enjoyed her, "She made him laugh. She was a feisty patient. She finally confronted him. 'I'm as healthy as I'm going to get,' she said. 'You don't want me to quit'."

Therapists may also have monetary motives. They might not want to let $10,000 a year "walk out the door." Some clients pay their therapists' mortgages and the therapists can't afford to lose them.

The article continues:

> "It's easy to spot therapy addicts. They're the ones who declare their emotions matter-of-factly and with pride: 'I'm angry and I feel good about that' or 'I'm upset, but that's okay.' They trumpet their therapy appointments—'Sorry, I can't do lunch tomorrow, I'm seeing my therapist'—and often serve as surrogate therapists for their friends. Therapy addicts don't say, 'I know just how you feel,' They say things like 'Could that have something to do with your mother?'"

Clients may become dependent on their therapists, or be afraid their therapists won't allow them to leave, or feel guilty that their therapists need and are attached to them, or feel obligated to them. If you want to terminate after only a few sessions and look for another therapist, don't let your therapist tell you that the reason you want to leave is that you're "resisting" therapy or "transferring" onto him the negative feelings you have for some other person in your life. If you're going to resist every therapist, you'll know that eventually. If you don't like the therapist, you're not likely to have a successful experience.

I've written in Chapter 1 about therapists I call "pathology hunters." They look for "sickness" in clients instead of looking for health. I recall a statement made by someone who was a clinical psychology intern when I was, who, responding to the model set for her by our instructors and supervisors, said, disappointedly, after a morning of attempting to interpret results of psychological tests she had given a 13 year old boy, "I've been sitting here all morning looking at this test material and I can't find anything wrong with this patient. I must be doing something wrong." She knew that she would not please her supervisor if she said that she thought the boy was basically "normal" when he asked for her report. Her supervisor had said to us both the week before "The only potential man has is for destruction." It seems that if students talk about disease and pathology, they're told they have good clinical ability to diagnose. To talk about health and positiveness is often not popular. Much of this negative interpretation can be harmful. For example, a pathology hunter might make the interpretation that someone is "withdrawn into a fantasy world," when, in fact, he is really "imaginative." Instead of saying that someone is "creative," he might be seen as "out of touch with reality." If your psychotherapist labels your behavior as "abnormal," he may be wrong. What the therapist considers normal or abnormal may have more to do with his perceptions than with your behavior. You've surely observed how often in courtroom battles psychiatrists for the defense are contradicted by psychiatrists for the prosecution on the matter of the defendant's sanity. You don't necessarily need therapy just because you phone a therapist for an appointment, but probably most therapists would believe you do, or they would say you do to get your business.

D.L. Rosenhan, professor of psychology and law at Stanford University, which has been called "the Harvard of the West," writing in 1973, tells about an experiment he conducted in which eight people, including himself, one graduate student, three psychologists, a pediatrician, a psychiatrist, a painter, and a woman who was a homemaker voluntarily presented themselves to the admitting staff of various psychiatric hospitals, pretending to have only one vague symptom. They had not given their actual names, and the mental health professionals reported that they worked in other occupations, but all other information given was accurate. They were, to their surprise, admitted to the hospitals without even being offered alternative plans to assist them. After admission they stopped pretending to have this symptom. But although many patients in these hospitals suspected that these researchers were "normal," and were probably journalists or professors "checking up on the hospital," the staff continued to believe they were mentally ill, interpreted their behavior as if it were related to the mental illness, and when they were discharged the diagnosis, the "label," remained, with the hospital records stating that the mental illness was "in remission," that is, the symptom was gone but the patient was expected to behave as a mentally ill person again in the future, that is, to be always mentally ill. Any diagnostic process that can so easily be in error cannot be very reliable. So, if the therapist labels your behavior "abnormal," he may be wrong. Or he may just want you as a paying customer.

I'm repeating what I've said about misdiagnosis of physical illnesses in chapter 1 because it's so important. Just because a psychiatrist is a medical doctor, *don't* assume that he is able to fully evaluate your problem and rule out all possible physical conditions that could be causing your symptoms. Psychiatrists are medical doctors, but they usually don't practice as "real doctors." They usually don't examine their clients physically. And they often leave their medical knowledge, skills, and practice behind them, preferring not to have stethoscopes, blood-drawing equipment, examining tables, or any medical equipment, except their prescription pads, and many prefer to believe that their clients' problems are "psychogenic," that is, caused by emotional disturbances. In fact, one psychiatrist I know about calls himself a "bio-psychiatrist," to convey that before he diagnoses or begins therapy with a client he carefully looks for physical illnesses that may be causing the symptoms. Even if a psychiatrist were to examine you physically, don't trust that his diagnosis is accurate. A high percentage of people have physical illnesses that are misdiagnosed, that are causing their distress, and they are committed to psychiatric hospitals. Unfortunately, even internists and other "real doctors," have an extraordinarily high rate of misdiagnosis. I know someone who consulted 37 physicians before her physical problem was diagnosed. All the other doctors had told her that she was emotionally disturbed—and they were wrong.

Changing may be painful, but there is no evidence that the more or the longer you suffer, the more successful your therapy will be. Freud said in 1919 "Cruel though it may sound, we must see to it that the patient's suffering, to a degree that is in some way or other effective, does not come to an end prematurely." Don't believe this! In an article titled "Suffering and Psychotherapy," Strupp says that clients have "been silent while undergoing protracted agonies." Classical psychoanalysts, following the teachings of Freud, believe that clients must suffer for a prolonged period of time and the analyst must not intervene to comfort them in any way, but must be detached, remote, unfeeling, not showing human concern. So much suffering is not therapeutic or humanitarian. A significant component of therapy involves using those human qualities that are helpful in dealing with a fellow human being's anxiety, distress, and unhappiness.

Why would a patient stay with a therapist if he's getting worse? According to Bergin: "Most people believe in expert, authority figures who have lots of diplomas on the wall." But psychotherapy clients, particularly, may:

> "tend to question their own judgment before questioning that of their therapist. They also tend to become dependent upon their expert as they get deeper into personal material. This makes it difficult for them to break off the relationship and start all over again with another therapist."

Some therapists have a lot of charisma, may be

attractive and appealing, so you can't always trust your feelings. Someone you "feel good" about may not be helpful. Or you may "fit" with him in unhealthy ways that don't bring out the best in you. And, if you've only had one therapist, you may not know you are being harmed. You'll read in this book the case of the successful attorney who was harmed for 12 years until, after talking with others, he finally realized what was happening to him. When he tried someone else who did help, he was then able to compare the differences.

Why do therapists allow other therapists to harm clients? It's not easy to report your co-worker, who sits in the next office, when you have to work with him every day, when you need your paycheck, and your boss wouldn't like that kind of trouble in his clinic. Even therapists who practice alone in their own businesses don't want to be labeled "whistle-blowers," "troublemakers," or "make waves." Making public the fact that some therapists harm their clients cannot be a good advertisement for psychotherapy. It's just not good for business. Even research about therapist behavior that portrays the therapist as a person, and that makes public the actual processes in therapy is unpopular, and any therapist who wants to do what is best for his career and for his relationships with colleagues does not irritate his fellow professionals.

In an article that covers the entire front page of the November 1982 *Monitor,* the newspaper of the American Psychological Association, titled "The spreading stain of fraud," mainly about fraud in research, Judith Swazey says that the "whistleblower" who exposes fraud in the psychological profession is the "deviant professional." She compares whistle-blowing to "treason, in that one undermines a country, and the other a profession, of its claim to independence from external control." She says that the professional accused of fraud may try to discredit the accuser to divert attention away from the fraud.

But I think that covering up the fact that some therapists actually harm their clients, denying that this is true, is truly bad for business. Psychotherapists are just people, and people can make mistakes and misjudgments. Instead of covering this up and losing credibility, appearing not to be trustworthy, we should find ways to acknowledge it and prevent it. One of those ways is to educate consumers about what they are buying. As E. Fuller Torrey believes "It is the obligation of all of us in the 'mental health' field to educate potential clients so they can better differentiate the helpers from the hucksters."

The consumers in this book were harmed in individual psychotherapy sessions. I think it's harder to be harmed in group therapy, where you have the benefit of the perceptions of others. Others may notice something you don't. And some clients are more likely to take action than others, stating their feelings about what's happening, and raising the consciousness of other participants. It's harder to fool all the people all the time. If one person says there's an elephant in the room, maybe there isn't. If two people say there's an elephant in the room, maybe they're both wrong. But, if three people say there's an elephant in the room, there probably is.

What do you do if you have been harmed? If your therapist is a licensed psychiatrist, psychologist, or psychiatric social worker, a complaint to the licensing board in the state in which he is practicing will be given to an "ethics committee" and you may feel empowered if you tell your story and also try to prevent others from having negative experiences with him and others who may harm clients. National professional organizations, such as the American Psychiatric Association, American Psychological Association, and National Association of Social Workers, (you'll find them listed in the Washington, D.C., phone book) also have ethics committees and procedures for handling your complaints. There are also state and local professional organizations, such as the New York State Psychological Association and others organized by counties or cities that are usually affiliated with the national groups, and which will also investigate your complaint. If more people filed complaints, there might not be so much abuse. I recently heard about a client suing not only the psychologist who had been her psychotherapist, but she also sued the others this man had worked with in a group practice, and she sued the state psychology licensing board that had given him his license to practice! You can bet that this state is busily trying to create ways to more carefully screen and continue to monitor the people they license.

If you find that the "therapist" does *not* have a license, then he is not violating rules of any licensing board or ethical standards of a professional group. But don't think he has nothing to lose or that you don't have a handle on this situation. Report your experience to the local District Attorney. Recently, I overheard a woman who was selling "healing crystals," which she said had powers to heal the body and distressed emotions, tell a customer that she uses them to "treat" her clients in her private practice as a "psychologist." When I asked her if, indeed, she was a psychologist, she answered "Yes." I then asked if she were licensed in California, the state in which she lives and works (although she sells crystals throughout the country), and she again answered that she was. I continued my interrogation, asking which school she'd attended, but I'd never heard of her supposed school. About a doctorate or master's degree, she said she didn't have one. I phoned the California psychology licensing board in Sacramento, and my suspicions that she was not a licensed psychologist were verified. I also discovered that she is *not* licensed in any state. Soon after my complaint she received a letter from the psychology licensing board telling her that she cannot legally call herself a psychologist in California (each state has its own licensing laws), and the case has been referred to the District Attorney in her locality. She is not only pretending to be a psychologist, but she is guilty of fraud because it has *not* been proven that crystals are healing.

If your rights are not defended by any of these actions, or even if they are, you may want to consult an attorney about a malpractice lawsuit.

Here are some examples of how a therapist can harm a client. They are statements from consumers about their experiences with harmful psychotherapists. These consumers have had one therapist who was helpful and another who was harmful. Clients with only one therapist don't have a comparison of therapist behavior—of personal characteristics of the therapist and of helpful technical factors. Without these contrasting experiences a client might believe that whatever the therapist did was right and that he is not to be criticized. Although I understand that the emotional nature of the psychotherapy situation can affect a client's perceptions, I believe that the statements that follow are *not* mere gossip or incorrect perceptions of emotionally distressed clients.

1. "He suggested that my wife and I split up, so we did. But a few months later we started living together again. Another harmful thing he did was when I terminated, he called my wife a few minutes after I left his office to tell her that he thought that she had a hysterical personality and that she was aborting her pregnancies and that she ought to come back and I ought to come back with her to see him together because her miscarriages were obviously a reaction to things that I was doing. What things? He answered 'Let's talk about it when you come back.' And when I became angry with him for this he said 'I'm glad to see you're getting in touch with your anger. That's exactly what I've been looking for all these years.' We never saw him again,

and my wife and I now have a lovely son."

2. "He put me on thorazine [powerful major tranquilizer with possible irreversible damaging side effects] when I was a teenager to help me sleep. He never told me if I couldn't take other pills with it. It was irresponsible. And the whole idea of trying to convince me that I was 'resistant.' He tried to deflate whatever confidence I had. That's something I've been particularly low on for most of my life. I had my mother and a lot of aunts and cousins who lived in the same building who all told me the same thing 'What you're thinking and you're saying is incorrect. It is not right.' I believe that I would have left my husband a lot sooner than I did because he kept making me believe that the reason the relationship didn't work was that it was my fault. Not only did he not push me in a forward direction, but as a result of my sessions with him I was more emotionally paralyzed than I might have otherwise been. He made me question my own judgment even further than I already had."

3. "When I was in therapy with him I began studying for a graduate degree in psychology. He decided that I shouldn't be doing that and terminated my therapy when I continued. I was in a terrible panic because I thought there was something terribly wrong with me and that he probably thought that I was positively unsuited for any work in this field. I later learned that his Freudian society had a rigid rule about clients studying psychology."

4. "He did almost everything harmful. He

served as a masculine hero for me and then used the power this gave him against me. He took over my life. He became the domineering parent. He made me believe that I could do nothing without consulting him. That his way was the best. That he was the best. I didn't even bother to bring in my own ideas. I came to accept everything he said as gospel. He even told me where to get my hair cut and where to buy my clothes. He hypnotized me, apparently. He was the god. He's not any different from the Moonies [cultist religious organization]. He got me to break with everyone who had a hold on me—parents, girlfriends, friends."

5. "He kissed me very hard on the mouth. And I had the sense that one little move and he would have gone crazy, and I was very upset. It wasn't helpful. I stopped seeing him. He also gave me advice that I should dress up and find a man and all would be well with me. He's a sexist."

6. "I had discussed my relationships with men in high school, that on several occasions when I liked a man I would call him and hang up. Somebody apparently was calling him and hanging up and he accused me of doing it. He would not accept that I was not doing it, and he kept insisting that I had feelings about him. And we spent many sessions talking about that. I just decided I wasn't going to see him anymore."

7. "She really didn't honor my own space. She had her own sort of program of the way therapy should be in terms of the mechanics and structure

of it. She wanted me to lie on a couch and free associate, and when I didn't she said I was 'resistant.' And the way she presented herself personally. She was pretty uptight and that was detrimental. I didn't feel safe and at home."

8. "I went in expecting that supportive third ear, which I didn't get. He didn't talk. It made me more depressed. I wanted somebody to respond to me. Not even to tell me that I was right, but to help me put some order into my life. He wanted to put me on valium [addictive and possibly harmful tranquilizer] and he thought that everything would be solved then."

9. "Her superior attitude really damaged me. I was just twenty years old, and I didn't have confidence in myself as a woman. She somehow had a way of making me feel my own inadequacies. It was the things she would say. One time she asked me why I didn't change in some way. She said 'You know, you're not a baby anymore,' which was just the thing I was struggling with, that I wasn't able to be mature enough about the problem. I knew I couldn't deal with the problem and I was embarrassed and humiliated that I couldn't handle what was going on. And having her say that confirmed this for me and didn't give me any hope that I could be any different. And she threw an interpretation in my face. I'm still angry at her. And she also told me, when she found that I was having sleeping problems, that, perhaps, I should think about leaving college. I was only a freshman. She said the pressure of school was too much for me and that maybe

my life wasn't there at school. Which was a crazy thing. My mother was dying. There were many other things that had nothing to do with school. I was getting all As in school. School wasn't the problem. Now, in retrospect, I've finished graduate school. She didn't know me at all."

10. "Twice he gave me sodium pentothal [hypnosedative barbiturate which is addictive and has possible irreversible harmful side effects including death]. It was very disorienting and I passed out. He didn't really use discretion. He should have seen that I wasn't doing well with it the first time. It was very unprofessional. And when I came to him in a crisis point and didn't have the money to pay him, he cast me out, literally opened the door. What kind of responsibility is that?"

11. "He recommended shock treatments [electricity directed through the brain]. He told me that there was a ninety percent chance that they would cure me. After a dozen it didn't do a thing. And he gave me no psychotherapy after, just tranquilizers. And he told me that therapy would never help me. He didn't know what the problem was and wasn't willing to admit he didn't know, so he made something up, like giving shock treatments for a phobia. He was inadequate. My father is a doctor and I respected a doctor's opinion. I did what he said. I had shock treatments. And when that didn't work he told me nothing could help me."

12. "Most of the times that I was there I was really angry at him. In addition to telling me what

to do and how to do it, he also reacted very poorly when I differed with him. If I questioned what he said, he got angry. He had an attitude that he was some sort of profound professor and I was a novice. And so most of the sessions we would be there exchanging anger. And what angered me even more is that I was paying for this. We were arguing and I wasn't getting anything out of it. There was no ultimate harm because I left him, but there could have been harm had I just said that this whole thing is not for me and just walked away and I never would have gotten any help from the therapist who did help me."

13. "It was nothing unethical or malicious, it was just that he didn't interact and I had expectations of what should be going on. And I came away from him feeling worse than when I went in, feeling that I had failed. And I had failed not once, but twice. I had tried two therapists. The first therapist I had stuck with and I had said 'I really have to try it.' I finally got up enough courage to get another therapist, and that one did not work either. I just felt there was no hope for me. I was just beyond help at that point. I said 'Well, I'll just have to function on my own. I can't get any help.' He was the expert in interpersonal relationships, and if I couldn't interact with him and communicate and gain something, that made me just completely ill, that I could not relate to him. Not only did I come in not feeling well, but I was worse because I went away feeling 'My God, I'm really terrible. I'm really sick. Because I can't even understand, I can't even

function with my therapist'."

14. "He undermined my self, and he sought to keep me in a dependent position. And he humiliated me in ways that I didn't understand until I left. He told me what to do. It was a parent-child relationship. He didn't give me a sense that I could do things, and he was punitive. And he did something that was absolutely dreadful. He had changed his office to a place farther from my job than the first office. I couldn't leave work early enough to keep my former hour and he refused to change my appointment time. I was screaming at him and he threatened to throw me out of his office if I didn't behave myself in a rational way. Talk about demeaning. It was total lack of respect for me as a person. It harmed me by not allowing me to have a sense of confidence in my ability to grow and to handle. I didn't have a sense that I could handle on my own."

15. "I had a new job and couldn't keep my appointment hour. He would not change my hour. He truly caused me a great deal of pain. When I terminated with him he told me that he had refused to change my time because he felt that life had always come very very easy to me and he was putting roadblocks in my path. It was no longer going to be easy. But at the end, after I left him, he said 'I think I have made a mistake.' At least he gave that."

16. "It was his personality and attitude. He was always trying to stay one step ahead of me, implying things that I did not say. And his lack of tolerance for people who didn't have the same view of the world."

CHAPTER 4

A Checklist To Rate Your Psychotherapist

There is too much mystery surrounding psychotherapy. It is time that we ask "Who are psychotherapists, and what do they do?" To what extent can psychotherapy be taught? How much of being a *good* psychotherapist is being the right person, and how much is knowing methods of psychotherapy and understanding personality dynamics?

Clients of psychotherapy are not often asked for their viewpoints of their psychotherapy or of their psychotherapists. Yet, it just makes sense to ask the client. And it is the client's experience that is most important, says psychologist Godfrey T. Barrett-Lennard, Director of the Centre for Studies in Human Relations, West Perth, Australia, who in the 1950s became the first major researcher of the client's perception of the therapeutic relationship, and is author of the "Relationship Inventory," which is still the most widely used questionnaire in this research. In these days of consumer consciousness, it is time that the client has a voice in evaluating his psychotherapist. The purpose of this book is to give clients that chance.

I hope you have learned about good psychotherapy and good psychotherapists from this book, and that you continue to educate yourself by talking with others and reading and attending lectures, and doing all you can to become an educated consumer.

I also hope you will create consumer groups in your towns for the purpose of gathering and distributing information about the process of psychotherapy, rating the competence of therapists and informing consumers about the best and the worst, offering a supportive network for consumers who've had negative experiences, and becoming a consumer advocate organization which will empower clients and be influential in bringing about a much better system for prevention of harm—the "psychological Food and Drug Administration" talked about in the first chapter.

To sum up what we know about finding a *good* psychotherapist who's likely to help you and not harm you, we recommend that you look for and avoid the following as you comparison shop. You will, of course, as we discussed in chapter 1, have already consulted a competent medical doctor and had a thorough physical exam to rule out physical problems that may be causing your symptoms. Remember that psychiatrists typically don't examine you physically and typically don't investigate possible physical causes for your distress. And even internists and other "real doctors" have a high rate of misdiagnosis of physical illness that can be causing your symptoms, so you may have to consult many doctors for an accurate diagnosis.

1. A helpful therapist is genuine, human, open, natural, offers a human connection, a relationship, is truthful about his thoughts and feelings, instead of tense, uneasy, closed, phony, inauthentic, playing roles, hiding behind a front. But, this is a professional, helping relationship. You're paying him to help you with your problems. He's not just a friend, and don't have an intensely personal relationship with him. If he tells you too much about his personal life, find another therapist. A therapist must share himself. He also might tell the client if he's had some experiences in common with him. But, he must know the limits. You're not there to listen to his experiences. Let's hope he understands himself, and he's reasonably secure, too. It would be wonderful if he has a sense of humor.

2. He must respect you, be interested in you, listen, be kind, warm and welcoming, instead of cold and distant or hostile. But, does this make him helpful if that's all he is? You're buying psychotherapy. You're not purchasing a friendship.

3. Do you feel understood? Does he know how you feel? Does he seem detached or too intellectual or analytical? He must have real feelings for your

distress and not just respond mechanically. If you don't feel that he really empathizes with you, if you don't feel his human response, then he can be compared to a musician who is technically proficient in his musical skills but lacks emotional expression in his work and is referred to by fellow musicians as a "technician," not a complimentary description. For example, I quote a well-known psychiatrist as he instructs psychotherapists in a textbook on how to interview clients, "The doctor can encourage free flow of expression by being responsive. He may nod or say, 'I understand'." Such programmed behavior is inauthentic, the client knows it, and it makes psychotherapists the target of much humor.

4. Responding in a healthy, human way seems to be just the usual kind of behavior for anyone. You don't want someone who will only say "Uh huh" or nod his head. I quote another psychiatrist whose book has been used as a standard psychotherapy training manual. He believes that the therapist must not "treat the patient in a conventional sense" because this "may cause the patient to regard the therapist as a person who should act in other conventional ways toward her." He adds that the therapist should avoid physical contact with the client, and "By his facial expression, the therapist must convey no embarrassment, fright, hostility or excitement." As I have said, a "professional" manner is necessary, but pretending not to think and feel and act like a person, pretending not to be a person, is senseless and silly. Of course, if you feel the therapist is too familiar with you—if

he attempts to approach you sexually—leave immediately!

5. A therapist must be active. He must talk to you, give you guidance and good advice, instead of sitting back in his chair and asking an occasional "How do you feel about that?" while you struggle alone to make your life work. But, he may be damaging if he gives you poor advice, or if he's too active and tells you what to do, takes over your life, and controls and dominates you instead of promoting your independence so you can master your world yourself. Some therapists encourage dependency in their clients, enjoying being needed and being powerful.

6. Anyone who can't tolerate criticism, who gets angry if you differ with him, who thinks he's an absolute authority and can never be wrong, is not the kind of person you want to spend many hours with, especially when you're taking this important journey into your feelings. You'd like him to be firm and to encourage you to change your behavior and your thinking, but in a sensitive and loving manner without being demanding or a dictator or trying to force you to change. Don't trust anyone who lets you think it's all right to do something unethical or irresponsible. That's not looking out for your best interest.

7. Along with having a healthy personality, a good psychotherapist must, of course, know how to be a psychotherapist. He can't just be a good person. He must be able to make an accurate diagnosis,

as much as that is at all possible. Many psychotherapists will assume you need psychotherapy just because you show up in their offices as possible clients. You may begin therapy because the therapist is a "pathology hunter," that is, has a bias toward interpreting behavior as "sick" instead of healthy, and labels your behavior as "abnormal," when this diagnosis is wrong. Or you may begin therapy because the therapist wants you as a paying customer. He must know theories of personality, understand you, and know how to use techniques of psychotherapy. And he should be flexible. For example, don't look for someone with a particular theoretical orientation or therapeutic technique. Don't look for a "psychoanalyst," who is someone who follows the teachings of Sigmund Freud and others who have their own versions of Freud's ideas. Don't look for a therapist who uses one of the "pop" or "fad" therapies, such as "est," "primal scream," or "rebirthing," etc. Instead, look for a *person* you can relate well to, who has good knowledge of *all* methods of psychotherapy, good technical skills, who understands you and your problem, and preferably has had successful experience working with many other clients with similar problems. What you want, ideally, is someone who is "eclectic," that is, he is *not* locked into any one "treatment modality," but rather uses whatever approaches and techniques are appropriate. To be truly eclectic he must have a thorough, broad base of learning, including all the various theories of personality and psychotherapy. Don't allow anyone to try to fit you and your problem into the rigid structure of one psychological theory or one way of treatment. If he rigidly follows rules of procedure, it may be because he's insecure and needs to follow these rules instead of creating a plan, with you participating, to treat you as a unique person with your particular problem. That's another requirement, that *you* must participate in deciding on what is called your "treatment plan." Clients have individual characteristics and needs that must be considered, and they should not be encouraged to perform certain "standard" behavior which conforms to the therapist's definition of what is "normal" and healthy. For example, some therapists encourage all of their clients to be aggressive or to get angry, when this has nothing to do with the problem or when it may even get the client into trouble, like being fired from a job or divorced. People who aren't open to a variety of ways of helping aren't going to learn all they can and aren't going to offer the best that is available for you and your specific problem. He shouldn't be preoccupied with constant interpretation and always analyzing your behavior so you neglect your outside reality and don't plan constructive action in your life. There's the old joke about two therapists who meet at an elevator and one says to the other "How are you?", and the other answers "What do you mean by that?" Be sure that what you learn about yourself is not just interesting, but that it is practical and relevant in your life. Many therapists concentrate on working out a systematic account of the client's emotional reactions and how they fit with the therapist's theoretical beliefs, says existential humanistic psychologist James Bugental, author of *Psychotherapy and Process,* and one of the founders of the Association for Humanistic Psychology. Bugental says that the client then has extensive supposed knowledge *about* himself, but little effective "inner vision," which is truly "insight." A therapist can tell you what he thinks are the reasons behind your feelings and actions, but no one can *give* you insight; you have to realize that yourself. Bugental refers to the "whodunit" strain in much therapy, when a therapist decides on what he thinks is a logical and coherent "interpretation" of your life and then carefully teaches this to you, expecting that you will change and be "cured." The futility of "second-hand insight" is obvious if you know people who can talk endlessly about their childhood, their "complexes," and their "defenses," but are not changed or helped. There is the joke about a man who's been in this kind of therapy for 10 years. A friend asks "After 10 years I suppose you're *cured?"* The client answers "No, but I *know* why I have problems." Also important is that a therapist use language you understand instead of technical jargon. If your therapist is a medical doctor and wants to prescribe "psychotropic" drugs—drugs used for psychological disorders—get another opinion before you agree. Major and minor tranquilizers, anti-depressants, sedatives, and hypnotics are not always the correct treatment, will not always definitely help you, and may produce unpleasant side effects. The practice of "shock treatments" is questionable, and you need to seriously research this treatment modality before making decisions about it. Consider all the issues very carefully and get lots of other professional opinions before you decide on these approaches. Don't admit yourself to a psychiatric hospital unless your situation is so extreme that there is no alternative. And, if you don't feel confidence in the therapist's capability, find someone else. If you've been seeing your therapist for many months with questionable results, tell him about your feelings and doubts and consult someone else. Therapy for you might be painful and difficult, but you *don't* necessarily have to suffer a lot. You must have an overall sense of progress, improvement, and comfort. If you stay with the therapist even though you are not benefiting, you are partly responsible for wasting your time and money. And if you've been in therapy for years, you may want to consider that this might be an expensive, non-productive dependency or addiction.

One of the consumers in this book sums all this up with:

> "If you're going to say that you're a therapist giving something to somebody, I think you have to *give* something. What you give is yourself, your strength, your ideas, or whatever is appropriate."

Remember that (1) Feeling "comfortable" with the therapist is very important, but not too comfortable or you may not be motivated to change. (2) "Fit" is important, getting along well with each other, but be on guard—if you fit too much it may not necessarily be a healthy or productive fit and may not bring out the best in you. (3) Credentials don't mean the therapist is competent and can't guarantee he will help you. (4) The therapist is *just* a person, too.

Now that you know what you'd like in a therapist, go shopping for one. Interview prospective therapists, bring someone whose judgment you trust to the interview with you if you want to, and discuss your interviews with people who can help you make good decisions, preferably people who have themselves had both helpful and unhelpful or harmful therapists. When you choose a therapist, have a legal, written contract with him as Ralph Nader suggests. Evaluate your choice and look for another therapist if you're not satisfied. And be hopeful. There is a good psychotherapist for you. There is someone who's right for you.

References

Adams, S., & Orgel, M. *Through the mental health maze, A consumer's guide to finding a psychotherapist, including a sample consumer/therapist contract.* Published in 1975 by: Public Citizen, Health Research Group, 2000 P Street NW, Washington, D.C. 20036.

Barrett-Lennard, G.T. *Dimensions of perceived therapist response related to therapeutic change.* Unpublished doctoral dissertation, University of Chicago, 1959.

Barrett-Lennard, G.T. "Dimensions of therapist response as causal factors in therapeutic change." *Psychological Monographs,* 1962, 76, No. 43 (Whole No. 562).

Barrett-Lennard, G.T. *Technical note on the 64-item revision of the Relationship Inventory.* Unpublished manuscript, University of Waterloo, Ontario, Canada, 1969.

Barrett-Lennard, G.T. "Empathy in human relationships: Significance, nature and measurement." *Australian Psychologist,* 1976, Vol. 2, 173-177.

Barrett-Lennard, G.T. The Relationship Inventory: Later developments and adaptations. JSAS *Catalog of Selected Documents in Psychology,* 1978, 8, 68. (Ms. No. 1732).

Bentley, J.C., DeJulio, S.S., Lambert, M.J., & Dinan, W. "The effects of traditional versus confrontive leadership styles in producing casualties in encounter group participants." Unpublished manuscript, Brigham Young University, Provo, Utah.

Bergin, A.E. "The effects of psychotherapy: Negative results revisited." *Journal of Counseling Psychology,* 1963, 10, 244-250.

Bergin, A.E. "Some implications of psychotherapy for therapeutic practice." *Journal of Abnormal Psychology,* 1966, 71, 235-246.

Bergin, A.E. "Further comments on psychotherapy research and therapeutic practice." *International Journal of Psychiatry*, 1967, 3, 317-323.

Bergin, A.E. "The evaluation of therapeutic outcomes." In A.E. Bergin & S.L. Garfield (Eds.), *Handbook of psychotherapy and behavior change* (1st ed.). New York: Wiley, 1971.

Bergin, A.E. "When shrinks hurt: Psychotherapy can be dangerous." *Psychology Today*, November 1975, p. 96.

Bergin, A.E., & Lambert, M.J. "The evaluation of therapeutic outcomes." In S.L. Garfield & A.E. Bergin (Eds.), *Handbook of psychotherapy and behavior change: An empirical analysis* (2nd ed.). New York: John Wiley & Sons, 1978.

Blackman, R. "Psychotherapy: How to Select Your Shrink." *Mademoiselle* 80, November 1974, p. 176 ff.

Buckley, P., Karasu, T., & Charles, E. "Psychotherapists view their personal therapy." *Psychotherapy: Theory, Research, Practice*, 1981, *18*, 299- 305.

Bugental, J.F.T. *Psychotherapy and process: The fundamentals of an existential-humanistic approach*. Reading, Massachusetts: Addison-Wesley, 1978.

Consumer Health and Nutrition Index. The Oryx Press, 2214 North Central at Encanto, Suite 103, Phoenix, Arizona 85004.

Cummings, N.A. "Prolonged (ideal) versus short-term (realistic) psychotherapy." *Professional Psychology*, November 1977, 491-501.

Ehrenberg, O., & Ehrenberg, M. "How, When, and Why to Fire Your Shrink." *New York Magazine*, May 12, 1975, p. 69ff.

Ehrenberg, O., & Ehrenberg, M. *The Psychotherapy Maze: A Consumer's Guide to Getting In and Out of Therapy* (revised edition). St. Louis, Missouri: Fireside, 1986.

Freud (1919). "Lines of advance in psycho-analytic therapy." *Standard Edition,* 12: 157-171. London: Hogarth Press, 1955.

Garfield, S.L., & Bergin, A.E. (Eds.) *Handbook of psychotherapy and behavior change: An empirical analysis* (2nd ed.). New York: John Wiley & Sons, 1978.

Garfield, S.L., & Bergin, A.E. (Eds.) *Handbook of psychotherapy and behavior change: An empirical analysis* (3rd ed.). New York: John Wiley & Sons, 1986.

Gillenkirk, J. "So You Think You Need a Psychiatrist." *Washingtonian,* November 1974, p. 122 ff.

Goleman, D. "Social Workers Vault into a Leading Role in Psychotherapy: Psychiatrists and Psychologists Defend Territory as Competition Increases." *Washington Post,* April 30, 1985.

Greenwald, H. Personal communication, 1971.

Greenwald, H., & Rich, E. *The happy person.* New York: Avon, 1984.

Grunebaum, H. "A study of therapists' choice of a therapist." *American Journal of Psychiatry,* 1983, *140,* 1336-39.

Grunebaum, H. "Harmful psychotherapy experience." *American Journal of Psychotherapy,* April 1986, Vol. XL, No. 2, 165-176.

Gurman, A.S. "The patient's perception of the therapeutic relationship." In A.S. Gurman & A.M. Razin (Eds.), *Effective psychotherapy: A handbook of research.* New York: Pergamon Press, 1977, 503-543.

Kaplan, R.E. "The dynamics of injury in encounter groups: Power, splitting, and the mismanagement of resistance." *International Journal of Group Psychotherapy,* 1982, 32 163-187.

Lambert, M.J., Bergin, A.E., & Collins, J.L. "Therapist-induced deterioration in psychotherapy." In A.S. Gurman & M. Razin (Eds.), *Effective psychotherapy: A handbook of research*. New York: Pergamon Press, 1977, 503-543.

Lambert, M.J., Shapiro, D.A., & Bergin, A.E. "The effectiveness of psychotherapy." In S.L. Garfield & A.E. Bergin (Eds.), *Handbook of psychotherapy and behavior change* (3rd ed.). New York: John Wiley & Sons, 1986, 157-211.

Lieberman, J.E., & Pewanick, C. "Consumer's guide to mental health services." In E. J. Lieberman (Ed.), *Mental health: The public health challenge*. Published in 1975 by: American Public Health Association, 1015 Eighteenth Street NW, Washington, D.C. 20036.

Lieberman, M.A., Yalom, I.D., & Miles, M.B. "Encounter: The leader makes the difference." *Psychology Today*, March 1973. (b)

Malan, D.H. *Toward the validation of dynamic psychotherapy*. London: Plenum Medical Book Company, 1976.

Minsky, T. "Prisoners of psychotherapy." *New York*, August 31, 1987, p.34.

Quinnett, Paul G. *The troubled people book: A consumer's guide to the world of psychologists and psychotherapists*. New York: Crossroad/Continuum, 1985.

Ricks, D.F. "Supershrink: Methods of a therapist judged successful on the basis of adult outcome of adolescent patients." In D. Ricks, M. Roff, & A. Thomas (Eds.), *Life history research in psychopathology* (Vol. III. Minneapolis: University of Minnesota Press, 1974.

Robinson, D. "Pick a therapist: Years and years on the wrong couch." *American Health*, Vol. 4, No. 5, p. 91, June 1985.

Rogers, C.R. "The necessary and sufficient conditions of therapeutic personality change." *Journal of Consulting Psychology*, 1957, 21, 95-103.

Rogers, C.R., & Dymond, R.F. (Eds.), Psychotherapy and personality change. Chicago: University of Chicago Press, 1954.

Rosehan, D.L. "On being sane in insane places." *Science,* January 19, 1973, 250-258.

Sachs, J.S. "Negative factors in brief psychotherapy: An empirical assessment." *Journal of Consulting and Clinical Psychology,* 1983, 51, 557-564.
Squires, S. "Shrunk by your shrink? Should you keep your therapist?" *American Health,* Vol. 5, No. 5, pp. 72-77. June 1986.

Striano, J. "Client perception of 'helpful' and 'not helpful' psychotherapeutic experiences" (Doctoral dissertation, The Fielding Institute, 1982). *Dissertation Abstracts International,* 1982, 43, 4303B. (University Microfilms No. 80-17, 382).

Striano, J. *Harmful psychotherapy.* Santa Barbara, California: Professional Press, 1987.

Striano, J. *Warning: Psychotherapists may be harmful to your mental health.* Santa Barbara, California: Professional Press, 1987.

Strupp, H.H. "Psychoanalytic failure." *Contemporary Psychoanalysis,* 1982, Vol. 18, No. 2, 235-251.

Strupp, H.H. "Suffering and psychotherapy." *Contemporary Psychoanalysis,* 1978, Vol. 14, No. 1, 73-97.

Strupp H.H. *Psychotherapists in action.* New York: Grune & Stratton, 1960.

Strupp, H.H. "Patient-doctor relationships: Psychotherapist in the therapeutic process." In A.J. Bachrach, (Ed.), *Experimental foundations of clinical psychology.* New York: Basic Books, 1962, 576-615.

Strupp, H.H. Personal communication, 1979.

Strupp, H.H., Fox, R.E., & Lessler, K. *Patients view their psychotherapy.* Baltimore: Johns Hopkins Press, 1969.

Strupp, H.H., & Hadley, S.W. "Specific versus nonspecific factors in psychotherapy: A controlled study of outcome." *Archives of General Psychiatry,* 1978, 36, 1125-1136.

Strupp, H.H., Hadley, S.W., & Gomes-Schwartz, B. *Psychotherapy for better or worse: The problem of negative effects.* New York: Jason Aronson, 1977.

Strupp, H.H., Wallach, M.S., & Wogan, M. "Psychotherapy experience in retrospect: Questionnaire survey of former patients and their therapists." *Psychological Monographs,* 1964, 78, No. 1. (11 Whole No. 588).

Swazey, J. "The spreading stain of fraud." *APA Monitor,* November 1982, p. 1.

Torrey, E.F. *Witchdoctors and psychiatrists: The common roots of psychotherapy and its future.* New York: Harper and Row, 1986.

Truax, C.B., & Mitchell, K.M. "Research on certain therapist interpersonal skills in relation to process and outcome." In A.W. Bergin & S.L. Garfield (Eds.), *Handbook of psychotherapy and behavior change: An empirical analysis.* New York: Wiley, 1971, 299-344.

Yalom, I.D. *The theory and practice of group psychotherapy* (2nd ed.). New York: Basic Books, 1975.

Yalom, I.D., & Lieberman, M.A. "A study of encounter group casualties." *Archives of General Psychiatry,* 1971, 25, 16-30.

CONSULTATION SERVICE

If you would like to discuss your search for a psychotherapist or your experience with a harmful psychotherapist, licensed clinical psychologist Dr. Judi Striano is available to talk with you on the telephone or in person, answering your questions and providing helpful information.

If you would like to be involved in research on helpful and harmful psychotherapists, your participation is welcome.

Telephone or write to Professional Press.

PROFESSIONAL PRESS
P.0. Box 50343
Santa Barbara, California 93150
805-565-1351

Also available by the author:

WARNING:
Psychotherapists
May be
Harmful
to Your
Mental Health

Judi Striano, Ph.D.

PROFESSIONAL PRESS
P.O. Box 50343
Santa Barbara, California 93150
(805) 565-1351 phone